P9-DFC-048

SEX

OPPOSING VIEWPOINTS®

Mary E. Williams, *Book Editor*

Bonnie Szumski, *Publisher*
Helen Cothran, *Managing Editor*

**OPPOSING
VIEWPOINTS®
SERIES**

GREENHAVEN PRESS
An imprint of Thomson Gale, a part of The Thomson Corporation

THOMSON
™
GALE

Detroit • New York • San Francisco • San Diego • New Haven, Conn.
Waterville, Maine • London • Munich

For more information, contact
Greenhaven Press
27500 Drake Rd.
Farmington Hills, MI 48331-3535
Or you can visit our Internet site at http://www.gale.com

Greenhaven Press anthologies primarily consist of previously published material taken from a variety of sources, including periodicals, books, scholarly journals, newspapers, government documents, and position papers from private and public organizations. These original sources are often edited for length and to ensure their accessibility for a young adult audience. The anthology editors also change the original titles of these works in order to clearly present the main thesis of each viewpoint and to explicitly indicate the opinion presented in the viewpoint. These alterations are made in consideration of both the reading and comprehension levels of a young adult audience. Every effort is made to ensure that Greenhaven Press accurately reflects the original intent of the authors included in this anthology.

LIBRARY OF CONGRESS CATALOGING-IN-PUBLICATION DATA
Sex / Mary E. Williams, book editor.
p. cm. — (Opposing viewpoints series)
Includes bibliographical references and index.
ISBN 0-7377-2959-7 (lib. : alk. paper) — ISBN 0-7377-2960-0 (pbk. : alk. paper)
1. Sex—United States. 2. Sexual ethics—United States. 3. Sex customs—United States. I. Williams, Mary E., 1960– . II. Opposing viewpoints series (Unnumbered)
HQ18.U5S45 2006
306.7—dc22   2005052578

Printed in the United States of America

"Congress shall make no law. . . abridging the freedom of speech, or of the press."

First Amendment to the U.S. Constitution

The basic foundation of our democracy is the First Amendment guarantee of freedom of expression. The Opposing Viewpoints Series is dedicated to the concept of this basic freedom and the idea that it is more important to practice it than to enshrine it.

Contents

Why Consider Opposing Viewpoints?

"The only way in which a human being can make some approach to knowing the whole of a subject is by hearing what can be said about it by persons of every variety of opinion and studying all modes in which it can be looked at by every character of mind. No wise man ever acquired his wisdom in any mode but this."

John Stuart Mill

In our media-intensive culture it is not difficult to find differing opinions. Thousands of newspapers and magazines and dozens of radio and television talk shows resound with differing points of view. The difficulty lies in deciding which opinion to agree with and which "experts" seem the most credible. The more inundated we become with differing opinions and claims, the more essential it is to hone critical reading and thinking skills to evaluate these ideas. Opposing Viewpoints books address this problem directly by presenting stimulating debates that can be used to enhance and teach these skills. The varied opinions contained in each book examine many different aspects of a single issue. While examining these conveniently edited opposing views, readers can develop critical thinking skills such as the ability to compare and contrast authors' credibility, facts, argumentation styles, use of persuasive techniques, and other stylistic tools. In short, the Opposing Viewpoints Series is an ideal way to attain the higher-level thinking and reading skills so essential in a culture of diverse and contradictory opinions.

In addition to providing a tool for critical thinking, Opposing Viewpoints books challenge readers to question their own strongly held opinions and assumptions. Most people form their opinions on the basis of upbringing, peer pressure, and personal, cultural, or professional bias. By reading carefully balanced opposing views, readers must directly confront new ideas as well as the opinions of those with whom they disagree. This is not to simplistically argue that everyone who reads opposing views will—or should—change his or her opinion. Instead, the series enhances readers' understanding of their own views by encouraging confrontation with opposing ideas. Careful examination of others' views can lead to the readers' understanding of the logical inconsistencies in their own opinions, perspective on why they hold an opinion, and the consideration of the possibility that their opinion requires further evaluation.

Evaluating Other Opinions

To ensure that this type of examination occurs, Opposing Viewpoints books present all types of opinions. Prominent spokespeople on different sides of each issue as well as well-known professionals from many disciplines challenge the reader. An additional goal of the series is to provide a forum for other, less known, or even unpopular viewpoints. The opinion of an ordinary person who has had to make the decision to cut off life support from a terminally ill relative, for example, may be just as valuable and provide just as much insight as a medical ethicist's professional opinion. The editors have two additional purposes in including these less known views. One, the editors encourage readers to respect others' opinions—even when not enhanced by professional credibility. It is only by reading or listening to and objectively evaluating others' ideas that one can determine whether they are worthy of consideration. Two, the inclusion of such viewpoints encourages the important critical thinking skill of objectively evaluating an author's credentials and bias. This evaluation will illuminate an author's reasons for taking a particular stance on an issue and will aid in readers' evaluation of the author's ideas.

It is our hope that these books will give readers a deeper understanding of the issues debated and an appreciation of the complexity of even seemingly simple issues when good and honest people disagree. This awareness is particularly important in a democratic society such as ours in which people enter into public debate to determine the common good. Those with whom one disagrees should not be regarded as enemies but rather as people whose views deserve careful examination and may shed light on one's own.

Thomas Jefferson once said that "difference of opinion leads to inquiry, and inquiry to truth." Jefferson, a broadly educated man, argued that "if a nation expects to be ignorant and free . . . it expects what never was and never will be." As individuals and as a nation, it is imperative that we consider the opinions of others and examine them with skill and discernment. The Opposing Viewpoints Series is intended to help readers achieve this goal.

David L. Bender and Bruno Leone,
Founders

Greenhaven Press anthologies primarily consist of previously published material taken from a variety of sources, including periodicals, books, scholarly journals, newspapers, government documents, and position papers from private and public organizations. These original sources are often edited for length and to ensure their accessibility for a young adult audience. The anthology editors also change the original titles of these works in order to clearly present the main thesis of each viewpoint and to explicitly indicate the opinion presented in the viewpoint. These alterations are made in consideration of both the reading and comprehension levels of a young adult audience. Every effort is made to ensure that Greenhaven Press accurately reflects the original intent of the authors included in this anthology.

Introduction

"If the people have no right to regulate sexuality then ultimately the institution of marriage is in peril."

—*Tom Minner, Focus on the Family*

"The [Supreme] Court's recognition that all women and men, regardless of their sexuality, have a constitutional right to privacy is a huge step forward."

—*Kim Gandy, National Organization for Women*

In 1998 a resident of Houston, Texas, called the police to report an alleged weapons disturbance at the apartment of John G. Lawrence. When police arrived and entered Lawrence's home, they found him having sex with a man, Tyron Garner. The two men were arrested, held overnight in jail, and fined two hundred dollars for violating Texas's Homosexual Conduct Law, an old statute that prohibited "deviate sexual intercourse," also referred to as sodomy. The two men sued the state of Texas, claiming that they had been denied privacy rights and equal protection under the law when they were arrested for engaging in consensual sex between adults.

The case, *Lawrence v. Texas*, was appealed to the U.S. Supreme Court. In its June 2003 ruling, all antisodomy laws were declared unconstitutional and unenforceable for consenting adults having noncommercial sex in private. Writing the court's majority opinion, Justice Anthony Kennedy declared that an adult's right to engage in consensual sex was protected under the term *liberty* in the Fourteenth Amendment, which states that "No State . . . shall deprive any person of life, liberty, or property, without due process [fair application] of law." Moreover, Kennedy asserted, "When homosexual conduct is made criminal by the law of the state, that declaration is in and of itself an invitation to subject homosexual persons to discrimination both in the public and in the private spheres."

Many observers noted that Texas's definition of "deviate sexual intercourse," which included both oral and anal sex, could have even made criminals out of some heterosexual married couples. But analysts argued that the law's intention was to prohibit such activity only between people of the same sex—and it was therefore a form of discrimination. If the police had found a man and a woman having oral sex, these critics pointed out, no arrests would have occurred.

The *Lawrence v. Texas* ruling ignited a heated debate over whether the government has the right to control or influence sexual activity between adults. History reveals that all societies have regulated sexual behavior with the intention of protecting the public from disease and other potentially destabilizing effects of unrestrained sexuality. For example, in 1873 the U.S. Congress passed the Comstock Act, which banned the mailing of "indecent and lascivious" materials, including books and pamphlets containing information about contraception and abortion. During this time, those who advocated sexual relationships outside of marriage were subject to arrest and imprisonment. In the twentieth century, however, the sexual revolution—a great transformation and liberalization of sexual mores—led to a wider availability of sexual information and a broader acceptance of nonmarital sexual activity. Yet some analysts have concerns, particularly after the abolition of all antisodomy laws in 2003, that the sexual revolution has gone too far.

Utah lawyer Camille Williams, for example, maintains that the state has a legitimate interest in passing laws that discourage sexual behavior outside of marriage. In striking down all antisodomy laws, she notes, the Supreme Court "appeared to ignore the fact that . . . private sexual activity has public consequences, some sexual practices are harmful, and . . . our society has the right, if not the obligation, to regulate sexual conduct to some degree." Without these laws, she contends, society bears the brunt of caring for large numbers of unmarried pregnant women and abandoned children as well as people suffering and dying from sexually transmitted diseases such as AIDS. In addition, she points out, such laws need not be overbearing or tyrannical: "We don't police private sexual conduct in an oppressive manner—for example, police do not peek through bedroom windows to ensure conformity of sexual practices." The intention of such laws had been largely to *dissuade* unhealthy sexual activity and to support commonly held moral standards—not to persecute sexual minorities. "We do not try to protect individuals from every dangerous or foolhardy activity," Williams explains, "but we do use the law to discourage some risky behaviors and to encourage safety and health measures."

Many contend, on the other hand, that the government should have no say in the intimate lives of adults. They maintain that antisodomy laws hearken back to a time when Americans held archaic ideas about sexuality, including the notion that sex served solely procreative purposes, that sexual pleasure was immoral, and that homosexuality was a vice. The abolishment of antisodomy laws is an acknowledgment that sexual mores have changed. As *New Republic* editor Andrew Sullivan put it: "I see a humane advance wherein men and women can express their sexuality unconstrained by the illogic and fear and misunderstanding that have bedeviled us in the past. In that respect, the ruling was a belated recognition of an established social change." Most importantly, says Glen A. Tobias of the Anti-Defamation League, the Supreme Court's ruling in *Lawrence v. Texas* "reaffirmed the principle that bigotry and fear may not be the basis for criminalizing private consensual conduct. . . . The decision is a ringing endorsement of the principles of individual liberty and freedom from discrimination and bigotry."

Lawrence v. Texas may indeed be seen as a pivotal Supreme Court ruling in the years to come. In May 2004, one year after this ruling, same-sex marriage became legal in Massachusetts. However, in November 2004, bans on same-sex marriage were approved by voters in eleven other states. Apparently the promoters of sexual liberation and the voices of traditional standards each continue to influence sexual norms. The authors in *Opposing Viewpoints: Sex* debate some of the most contentious issues concerning sexuality in the following chapters: Are Sexual Ethics Eroding? What Sexual Norms Should Society Uphold? How Should Sex Education Be Conducted? Are Some Sexual Behaviors Unacceptable? This volume offers an intriguing overview of several current debates concerning sexuality and sexual values.

CHAPTER 1

Are Sexual Ethics Eroding?

Chapter Preface

In the 1960s and 1970s, many observers heralded America's sexual revolution for its endorsement of more liberal standards concerning nonprocreative sex. The advent of the birth control pill in 1960 increased access to reliable contraception and thus afforded women unprecedented control over their sexual and reproductive lives. In addition, sexuality and gender became focal points around which new political movements—including the women's liberation movement and the gay and lesbian rights movement—were organized. By the end of the twentieth century, an increased acceptance of nonmarital sex, cohabitation, single parenthood, homosexuality, and abortion was often cited as the legacy of the sexual revolution in the United States and in other Western nations.

Many of today's analysts, however, wonder whether the sexual revolution has gone too far. Conservative critics often argue that sexual liberation has separated sexual pleasure from committed love, creating a disturbing erosion of sexual ethics and leading to higher rates of teen pregnancy, sexually transmitted diseases, marital infidelity, divorce, and loneliness. Columnist Cal Thomas maintains that "the progeny of the *Playboy* philosophy—which said men did not have to limit their sex drive to their wives but could plunder whatever woman would allow them—is brokenness, depression, addiction, and, in some cases, suicide. . . . The throwing off of all restraints has produced a culture without rules, without signposts and without meaning." One remedy for this cultural alienation, many contend, is to reinforce the time-honored values that allow sexual activity only within the confines of traditional marriage.

Some progressive observers also acknowledge that the sexual revolution has had its shortcomings, such as the exploitation of sexuality in the advertising and entertainment industries. As Sarah Van Gelder, executive director of the Positive Futures Network, states, "The mysteries of sexual ecstasy are trivialized—all is laid out in magazines and videos. There is little discussion of the effects of inundating the culture with superficial images of sexuality and associating those images with consumerism, violence, and exploitation rather than love and creativity." Yet many would not want to return to the days before the sexual revolution, when lifestyle and relationship choices were extremely limited, especially for women. Syndicated columnist Isadora Allman recalls growing up in the 1950s, when all women were expected to marry young: "If you didn't marry or have children . . . you were something weird, like Marion the Librarian. If you were a career gal, sexless, peculiar." But today, notes Allman, "a person can be a nurse or an astronaut, male or female, can be monogamous or not, be with a person of the same sex or not, marry several times, not marry at all, have children whether you're married or not. There are more choices for making a life that's personally more rewarding."

Whether the sexual revolution has led to an erosion of sexual ethics is the subject of the following chapter, in which analysts discuss the legacy of sex researcher Alfred C. Kinsey, current attitudes toward sexual pleasure and sexual rights, and the advent of same-sex marriage.

"When Kinsey tore the mystery of love from human sexuality, he abandoned us all to a sexually broken world."

Alfred Kinsey's Research Has Undermined Sexual Morality

Sue Ellin Browder

In the following viewpoint Sue Ellin Browder contends that Alfred C. Kinsey's seriously flawed research on human sexuality led to a sexual revolution that damaged American society. According to Browder, Kinsey's startling conclusions about the sexuality of Americans—including the claim that nonmarital sex and homosexuality were commonplace—were based on deeply skewed statistics. American culture, however, has largely embraced Kinsey's misinformation, which in turn has led to a general decline in sexual morality. Investigative journalist Browder is coauthor of *101 Secrets a Good Dad Knows*.

As you read, consider the following questions:

1. How many varieties of sexually transmitted diseases exist today, according to Browder? How many were widely reported in the 1950s?
2. According to the author, what percentage of men did Kinsey claim to be guilty of sex crimes?
3. In what way has Kinsey's research damaged the American legal system, in Browder's opinion?

Sue Ellin Browder, "Kinsey's Secret," *Crisis*, vol. 22, May 2004, pp. 13–14, 16–17.

It's now more than 50 years since the revolution began. Sexual "liberation" has been endlessly ballyhooed by the national media, promoted in the movies, embraced by *Playboy* guys and *Cosmo* girls as a freedom more delicious than Eden's apple. No American under 40 can honestly remember a time when sex on TV was taboo, when "living together" meant married, when "gay" meant happy, and when almost every child lived with both parents.

If truth be told, the revolution has been a disaster. Before the push to loosen America's sexual mores really got under way in the 1950s, the only widely reported sexually transmitted diseases in the United States were gonorrhea and syphilis. Today we have more than two dozen varieties, from pelvic inflammatory disease (which renders more than 100,000 American women infertile each year) to AIDS (which presently infects 42 million people worldwide and has already killed another 23 million). According to a report by scientists at the National Cancer Institute, a woman who has three or more sex partners in her lifetime increases her risk of cervical cancer by as much as 1,500 percent. In another finding that runs contrary to all that the sex researchers preached, a survey at the University of Chicago's National Opinion Research Center showed that *married* men and women, on average, are sexually happier than unwed couples merely living together. And even if live-in couples do marry, they're 40 to 85 percent more likely to divorce than those who go straight to the altar.

So what happened? Was science simply wrong? Well, not exactly—the truth is more complicated than that.

And much more interesting.

A Con Man

Alfred C. Kinsey had a secret. The Indiana University zoologist and "father of the sexual revolution" almost single-handedly redefined the sexual mores of everyday Americans. The problem was, he had to lie to do it. The weight of this point must not be underestimated. The science that launched the sexual revolution has been used for the past 50 years to sway court decisions, pass legislation, introduce sex education into our schools, and even push for a redefinition of marriage.

Kinseyism was the very *foundation* of this effort. If his science was flawed—or worse yet, an outright deception— then our culture's attitudes about sex are not just wrong morally but scientifically as well.

Let's consider the facts. When Kinsey and his coworkers published *Sexual Behavior in the Human Male* in 1948 and *Sexual Behavior in the Human Female* in 1953, they turned middle-class values upside down. Many traditionally forbidden sexual practices, Kinsey and his colleagues proclaimed, were surprisingly commonplace; 85 percent of men and 48 percent of women said they'd had premarital sex, and 50 percent of men and 40 percent of women had been unfaithful after marriage. Incredibly, 71 percent of women claimed their affair hadn't hurt their marriage, and a few even said it had helped. What's more, 69 percent of men had been with prostitutes, 10 percent had been homosexual for at least three years, and 17 percent of farm boys had experienced sex with animals. Implicit in Kinsey's report was the notion that these behaviors were biologically "normal" and hurt no one. Therefore, people should act on their impulses with no inhibition or guilt.

Flawed Research

The 1948 report on men came out to rave reviews and sold an astonishing 200,000 copies in two months. Kinsey's name was everywhere from the titles of pop songs ("Ooh, Dr. Kinsey") to the pages of *Life*, *Time*, *Newsweek*, and the *New Yorker*. Kinsey was "presenting facts," *Look* magazine proclaimed. He was "revealing not what should be but what is." Dubbed "Dr. Sex" and applauded for his personal courage, the researcher was compared to Darwin, Galileo, and Freud.

But beneath the popular approbation, many astute scientists were warning that Kinsey's research was gravely flawed. The list of critics, Kinsey biographer James H. Jones observes, "read like a Who's Who of American intellectual life." They included anthropologists Margaret Mead and Ruth Benedict; Stanford University psychologist Lewis M. Terman; Karl Menninger, M.D. (founder of the famed Menninger Institute); psychiatrists Eric Fromm and Lawrence

Kubie; cultural critic Lionel Trilling of Columbia University, and countless others.

By the time Kinsey's volume about women was published, many journalists had abandoned the admiring throngs and joined the critics. Magazine articles appeared with titles like "Is the Kinsey Report a Hoax?" and "Love Is Not a Statistic." *Time* magazine ran a series of stories exposing Kinsey's dubious science (one was titled "Sex or Snake Oil?").

That's not, of course, to say that the Kinsey reports contain no truth at all. Sexuality is certainly a subject worthy of scientific study. And many people *do* pay lip-service to sexual purity while secretly behaving altogether differently in their private lives.

Nevertheless, Kinsey's version of the truth was so grossly oversimplified, exaggerated, and mixed with falsehoods, it's difficult to sort fact from fiction. Distinguished British anthropologist Geoffrey Gorer put it well when he called the reports propaganda masquerading as science. Indeed, the flaws in Kinsey's work stirred up such controversy that the Rockefeller Foundation, which had backed the original research, withdrew its funding of $100,000 a year. A year after the book on female sexuality came out, Kinsey himself complained that almost no scientist outside of a few of his best friends continued to defend him.

So, what were the issues the world's best scientists had with Kinsey's work? The criticism can be condensed into three devastating points.

Problem #1: Humans as Animals

Before he began studying human sexuality, Kinsey was the world's leading expert on the gall wasp. Trained as a zoologist, he saw sex purely as a physiological "animal" response. Throughout his books, he continually refers to the "human animal." In fact, in Kinsey's opinion, there was no moral difference between one sexual outlet and any other. In our secular world of moral relativism, Kinsey was a radical sexual relativist. As even the libertarian anthropologist Margaret Mead accurately observed, in Kinsey's view there was no moral difference between a man having sex with a woman— or a sheep.

In his volume about women, Kinsey likened the human orgasm to sneezing. Noting that this ludicrous description left out the obvious psychological aspects of human sexuality, Brooklyn College anthropologist George Simpson observed, "This is truly a monkey-theory of orgasm." Human beings, of course, differ from animals in two very important ways: We can think rationally, and we have free will. But in Kinsey's worldview, humans differed from animals only when it came to procreation. Animals have sex *only* to procreate. On the other hand, human procreation got little notice from Kinsey. In his 842-page volume on female sexuality, motherhood wasn't mentioned once.

Problem #2: Skewed Samples

Kinsey often presented his statistics as if they applied to *average* moms, dads, sisters, and brothers. In doing so, he claimed 95 percent of American men had violated sex-crime laws that could land them in jail. Thus Americans were told they had to change their sex-offender laws to "fit the facts." But, in reality, Kinsey's reports never applied to average people in the general population. In fact, many of the men Kinsey surveyed were actually prison inmates. Wardell B. Pomeroy, Kinsey co-author and an eyewitness to the research, wrote that by 1946 the team had taken sexual histories from about 1,400 imprisoned sex offenders. Kinsey never revealed how many of these criminals were included in his total sample of "about 5,300" white males. But he did admit including "several hundred" male prostitutes. Additionally, at least 317 of Kinsey's male subjects were not even adults, but sexually abused children.

Piling error on top of error, about 75 percent of Kinsey's adult male subjects volunteered to give their sexual histories. As Stanford University psychologist Lewis M. Terman observed, volunteers for sex studies are two to four times more sexually active than non-volunteers.

Kinsey's work didn't improve in his volume on women. In fact, he interviewed so few average women that he actually had to redefine "married" to include any woman who had lived with a man for more than a year. This change added prostitutes to his sample of "married" women.

In the December 11, 1949, *New York Times*, W. Allen Wallis, then chairman of the University of Chicago's committee on statistics, dismissed "the entire method of collecting and presenting the statistics which underlie Dr. Kinsey's conclusions." Wallis noted, "There are six major aspects of any statistical research, and Kinsey fails on four."

Outlandish Claims

Kinsey's sensational "research" turns out to be not scientific at all, but outright fraud. In order to undo traditional moral norms, Kinsey had to perpetrate the lie that all kinds of perverse sexual practices were "normal." According to Kinsey, anything goes: promiscuity, pornography, prostitution, adultery, sodomy, pedophilia, group sex, sadomasochism, even incest. To support his outlandish claims, Kinsey intentionally skewed his population sample by secretly stacking his "research" with selected cohorts from the most sexually disordered populations: rapists, child molesters, prison inmates, homosexual activists, the "feeble minded," and prostitutes.

Judith Reisman, *New American*, November 15, 2004.

In short, Kinsey's team researched the most exotic sexual behavior in America—taking hundreds if not thousands of case histories from sexual deviants—and then passed off the behavior as sexually "normal," "natural," and "average" (and hence socially and morally acceptable).

Problem #3: Faulty Statistics

Given all this, it's hardly surprising that Kinsey's statistics were so seriously flawed that no reputable scientific survey has ever been able to duplicate them.

Kinsey claimed, for instance, that 10 percent of men between the ages of 16 and 55 were homosexual. Yet in one of the most thorough nationwide surveys on male sexual behavior ever conducted, scientists at Battelle Human Affairs Research Centers in Seattle found that men who considered themselves exclusively homosexual accounted for only 1 percent of the population. In 1993, *Time* magazine reported, "Recent surveys from France, Britain, Canada, Norway and Denmark all point to numbers lower than 10 percent and tend to come out in the 1 to 4 percent range." The incidence of homosexuality among adults is actually "between 1 and 3 percent," says University of Delaware sociology and criminal justice professor Joel Best, author of *Damned Lies and Statistics*. Best observes, however, that gay and lesbian activists prefer to use Kinsey's long-discredited one-in-ten figure "because it suggests that homosexuals are a substantial minority group, roughly equal in number to African Americans—too large to be ignored."

Not surprisingly, Kinsey's numbers showing marital infidelity to be harmless also never held up. In one *Journal of Sex and Marital Therapy* study of infidelity, 85 percent of marriages were damaged as a result, and 34 percent ended in divorce. Even spouses who stayed together usually described their marriages afterwards as unhappy. Atlanta psychiatrist Frank Pittman, M.D., estimates that among couples who have been married for a long time and then divorce, "over 90 percent of the divorces involve infidelities."

Speaking at a 1955 conference sponsored by Planned Parenthood, Kinsey pulled another statistical bombshell out of his hat. He claimed that of all pregnant women, roughly 95 percent of singles and 25 percent of those who were married secretly aborted their babies. A whopping 87 percent of these abortions, he claimed, were performed by bona fide doctors. Thus he gave scientific authority to the notion that abortion was already a common medical procedure—and should thus be legal.

Living with the Wreckage

When *Reader's Digest* asked popular sex therapist Ruth Westheimer what she thought of Kinsey's misinformation, she reportedly replied, "I don't care much about what is correct and is not correct. Without him, I wouldn't be Dr. Ruth."

But Kinsey's deceptions *do* matter today, because we're still living with the Kinsey model of sexuality. It permeates our entire culture. As Best observes, bad statistics are significant for many reasons: "They can be used to stir up public outrage or fear, they can distort our understanding of our world, and they can lead us to make poor policy choices."

In a 1951 *Journal of Social Psychology* study, psychology students at the University of California, Los Angeles, were divided into three groups: Some students took an intensive nine-week course on Kinsey's findings, while the other two groups received no formal Kinsey instruction. Afterward, the students took a quiz testing their attitudes about sex. Compared with those who received no Kinsey training, those steeped in Kinseyism were seven times as likely to view premarital sex more favorably than they did before and twice as likely to look more favorably on adultery. After Kinsey, the percentage of students open to a homosexual experience soared from 0 to 15 percent. Students taught Kinseyism were also less likely to let religion influence their sexual behavior and less apt to follow sexual rules taught by their parents.

Influencing Court Decisions

Kinsey's pseudoscience arguably did the most damage through our court systems. That's where attorneys used the researcher's "facts" to repeal or weaken laws against abortion, pornography, obscenity, divorce, adultery, and sodomy. In the May 1950 issue of *Scientific Monthly*, New York City attorney Morris Ernst (who represented Kinsey, Margaret Sanger, the American Civil Liberties Union, and Planned Parenthood) outlined his ambitious legal plan for Kinsey's findings. "We must remember that there are two parts to law," Ernst said. One was "the finding of the facts" (Kinsey's job); the other was applying those findings in court (Ernst's job). Noting that the law needed more tools "to aid in its search for the truth," the attorney argued for "new rules," under which "facts" like Kinsey's would be introduced into court cases in the same way judges allowed other scientific tools, such as fingerprints, lie-detector results, and blood tests. The inexhaustible Ernst also urged the courts to revise laws concerning the institution of marriage.

The legal fallout from Kinsey's work continues. The U.S. Supreme Court's historic decision [in 2003] striking down sodomy laws was the offshoot of a long string of court cases won largely on the basis of Kinsey's research. And 50 years of precedents set by Kinsey's "false 10 percent" are now being used in states like Massachusetts to redefine marriage.

Inspired by the first Kinsey report, Hugh Hefner founded *Playboy* in 1953. A decade later, Helen Gurley Brown turned

Cosmopolitan into a sex magazine for women. Even today magazines like *Self* and *Glamour* continue to quote Kinsey with respect, never acknowledging the grave errors riddling his research. An estimated 30,000 Web sites offer pornography, and U.S. producers churn out 600 hard-core adult videos each month. Although reliable figures are difficult to come by, the U.S. sex industry pulls in an estimated $2.5 billion to $10 billion a year. Clearly, we're living Kinsey's legacy.

In his book *The End of Sex*, an obituary of the sexual revolution, *Esquire* contributor George Leonard accurately observed that "wherever we have split 'sex' from love, creation, and the rest of life . . . we have trivialized and depersonalized the act of love itself." Treasuring others solely for their sexuality strips them of their humanity. When Kinsey tore the mystery of love from human sexuality, he abandoned us all to a sexually broken world. It's time to heal.

"[Kinsey] taught us not to be so judgmental, of ourselves or others, and that's a lesson we can all continue to learn."

Alfred Kinsey's Research Has Increased Awareness About Human Sexuality

Marjorie Ingall

The work of Alfred C. Kinsey transformed American society by fostering a fuller understanding of human sexuality, writes Marjorie Ingall in the following viewpoint. Kinsey's research on women is especially noteworthy for confronting stereotypes about female sexuality and for ushering in a revolution that granted women more control over their sex lives, notes Ingall. The author acknowledges that Americans are often bombarded by shallow, glitzy images of sexuality today, but she is ultimately grateful to Kinsey for helping to create a world that is more open to sexual diversity. Ingall, a frequent contributor to *Glamour* magazine, is the coauthor of *Smart Sex*.

As you read, consider the following questions:

1. In Kinsey's 1953 book, *Sexual Behavior in the Human Female*, what percentage of American women reported having had premarital sex?
2. What approach did Kinsey take when he interviewed people, according to Ingall?
3. According to the author, what question did Kinsey's female interviewees often ask him?

Take a moment and imagine a world in which you never discussed your sex life. Not even with your best friends. No one you knew, except maybe your doctor, ever uttered the words *penis* and *vagina*. Imagine no MTV, no birth control pill, no Barbie, no nudity in movies or magazines, no girl sitting next to you on the bus yammering into her cell phone about her hot date.

Now open your eyes and look around. Somewhere, probably right in front of you, there is . . . sex, sex and more sex. Think about it: We've seen two contestants on *Survivor: The Amazon* get naked for peanut butter and chocolate; we've glimpsed almost as much of Christina Aguilera's and Lil' Kim's bodies as their gynecologists have. For heaven's sake, we have sat in our local cineplex and watched a guy have sex with a pie.

And all these changes might never have happened without the publication, way back in 1953, of one little book. Actually, it wasn't so little. *Sexual Behavior in the Human Female*, by Alfred C. Kinsey, Ph.D., a professor at Indiana University in Bloomington, was the first scientific report on women's sex lives. It took more than 15 years to prepare and involved 5,940 interviews. Among the findings: About half of American women reported having had premarital sex; as many as 14 percent of women ages 20 to 35 said they'd had a sexual experience with another woman; 26 percent of married women had had affairs; 62 percent of women said they'd masturbated.

The Initial Reaction to Kinsey

The reaction: Many media outlets (including *Glamour* and *Newsweek*) hailed the study, but some (including *Time* and *Cosmopolitan*) questioned its accuracy and said its findings "favor loose morals." A New York congressman called many of the women who were interviewed "frustrated, neurotic outcasts of society." (The majority were college-educated Midwestern white women. In fact, Kinsey has been criticized for not interviewing a more scientific, diverse sample.) The congressman also accused the book of "contributing to the depravity of a whole generation . . . and to the misunderstanding and the confusion about sex." One woman proclaimed to *The Scarsdale Inquirer* that Kinsey "has opened a veritable Pandora's box of incalculable evil such as the world has never known!" Gracious!

Thankfully, today's experts disagree. "Taking away the taboo of even discussing sex has allowed couples to talk more comfortably about what they want and don't want," says Gail Saltz, M.D., assistant professor of psychiatry at New York–Presbyterian Weill Cornell Medical Center in New York City. The flip side of all this openness, however, is a culture that titters and titillates and hints at sex all the time.

Obsessed with Sex?

So what have we gained? If we are freer to talk about sex (shout it from billboards, even), are we any more satisfied? Is private life any easier in our sex-saturated culture?

When I watch all those gyrating perfect bodies in *The Matrix Reloaded*'s, rave orgy and all those girls licking their glossy lips over bachelors on reality shows, I can't help thinking they've turned sexuality into shallow performance art, separating it from what it really is: an intimate, physical act.

"We're obsessed with the image of sex at the expense of our own satisfaction," says Lily Burana, a former exotic dancer and the author of *Strip City*. "We're all supposed to be physically perfect, gorgeously dressed, young and single." In our celebrity-obsessed culture, women tend to compare and despair. We worry about whether we're getting enough sex or the right kind of sex. It seems impossible to keep up with the [Catherine] Zeta-Joneses. "I've been in *Playboy* and I've been a stripper," says Burana, "and I still feel unentitled to things because I'm not a size 0!"

I confess, I'm deeply ambivalent. I'm glad I didn't marry the first guy I slept with and equally glad that I slept with that guy. (He was a blond, blue-eyed actor with great shoulders and not such a great head on them—exactly the kind of boy it's fine to practice on and less fine to spend your life with.) I'm glad I could read *Our Bodies, Ourselves* when I was a teenager and learn that vaginal discharge can be normal; if I'd been a sexually active young adult in the fifties, I'd never have found that information in your average bookstore. I'm glad I have access to birth control and abortion. I'm glad that my brother, a gay man, can live his life in the open without going to jail for it.

Yet I bet I'm more sexually self-conscious than my grandmother was 50 years ago, when the Kinsey report shocked the world, because I'm bombarded with more images of perfect naked bodies than she ever was. Unlike my grandma, I know entirely too much about Sting's tantric sex life. Imagining that he is perpetually using his yoga-toned body to bring Trudie to the brink of ecstasy makes me wonder. Why am *I* not having tantric sex right now? To get some perspective on all this openness, I talked to a few pioneering women whose closed-door conversations with Kinsey unleashed the rowdy, rousing sexual dialogue we are all part of today.

The Silence Breakers

It wasn't easy to find Kinsey's interviewees—he was so zealous about protecting their privacy that most of their identities have never been revealed. He didn't write down their answers verbatim; instead, he used his own secret code, the key to which was memorized by his four interviewers. (To ensure the survival of the code, the four never traveled in an airplane together!) Their data were both precious and extremely private; these were among the first average, healthy American women ever to talk to a researcher about oral sex,

Pett. © by Joel Pett. Reproduced by permission.

orgasms, infidelity and their same-sex experimentation.

What persuaded these women to be so open? For some, the appeal was Kinsey himself, a former zoology professor who liked classical music. "I found him charming," says Alice Ginott, Ph.D., now 79, who was interviewed when she was 19. She didn't know what to expect once the door to the interview room closed and she was sitting face-to-face with Kinsey in a room that was bare other than the table between them. Each interview included up to 521 questions, starting with such topics as family background, education and religion. "I trusted him," Ginott says. Gradually the questions took a more intimate turn. They focused on a woman's earliest orgasm, her attitude toward nudity, her erogenous zones, how many sex partners she'd had, the positions she'd tried. If the woman was a virgin, the interview took about an hour. If she'd had more experience, it might take as long as two hours. "Boys would come and sit outside the interview room," Ginott remembers. "And if a girl was inside for two hours, that's the girl they became interested in!"

Kinsey's Interviewing Technique

Kinsey always acted as though his interviewees had done everything. For instance, he'd ask, "When did you begin sexual relations before marriage?" leaving it to the woman to protest, "But I never had sex before marriage!" Today social scientists would be horrified by this technique, but it may have been the best way to get women to confess their sexual secrets.

Ginott believes Kinsey probably made many women feel more comfortable about sex. In fact, a common question interviewees would ask Kinsey was, "Am I really normal, Doctor?"

Kinsey also interviewed Helen Wallin D'Amico, now 84, who was his secretary at the time. "The questions just had a flow, and I forgot where I was and what I was doing," D'Amico says. "Afterward, I was shocked at what I'd said!" But she wasn't surprised by the book's findings. "I thought it was a portrait of reality," she shrugs. "Sex is not a dirty word, and Kinsey wanted to get it out in the open."

Not everyone who sat through Kinsey's survey remembered it as fondly as Ginott and D'Amico did. Back in 1953, *Glamour* published an article by Beatrice Schapper, who'd been interviewed by Kinsey in 1947. She'd tracked down a number of interviewees and found that many refused to discuss their experience: "A millinery saleslady said, 'Going through *that* once was enough!' and slammed down the phone," Schapper wrote. "Still another snapped, 'There's been too much excitement over Kinsey's work already. I will not add to it!'" But plenty of women spoke positively about their meetings with Kinsey, including one who was 89 when she talked to him and wished she'd had such frank conversation earlier: "Had I been really free in my feelings . . . I know now that my life would have been richer and happier."

An Empowered View

Indeed, Kinsey helped usher in a far more empowered view of sexuality for women. In an era when experts still believed in the "mature" (vaginal) orgasm and the "immature" (clitoral) orgasm, Kinsey's research gave women a more honest take on what was normal. Today most of us feel confident that an orgasm is an orgasm and that you can have a great one without a penis in the vicinity. Kinsey also taught us that women reach their sexual peak later than men do. (Yay for me! Condolences to my husband.) Such knowledge is as essential now as it was then—how else can we be in charge of our own sexual joy?

Ask today's sex gurus for other reasons Kinsey's 5,000-plus interviews still hold a special place in sexual history and they'll give you an earful: "If it weren't for Kinsey," says Cindy Pearson, executive director of the National Women's Health Network in Washington, D.C., "women would still be getting this oversimplified message that their whole sexuality should consist of a physical relationship with one man, and vaginal intercourse is the most important way to derive satisfaction." Kinsey also taught us that "normal" is a big tent. There's a vast panoply of turn-ons among American women, he found. And he taught us not to be so judgmental, of ourselves or others, and that's a lesson we can all continue to learn.

Where Are Women Headed Now?

Still, our cultural overload of sex could lead to a new kind of performance anxiety. "Studies show that kids get desensitized by violent video games, and I wonder whether the same is true about sexual behavior," says Dr. Saltz. She may be right. We see the same glossy, synthetic images over and over, which I fear makes us feel that they're what sex is all about. I'm still searching for depictions of older people's sexuality, of people with imperfect bodies making love. Right now we're on the verge of a new kind of sexual tyranny: the domination of the seemingly perfect.

Here's something to work on over the *next* 50 years: Let's try to stop comparing ourselves to the sexual icons all around us. We've become so susceptible to images that we may not value the realness in our own bedrooms. And we may not work hard enough at fixing our own sex lives because we see them as too pathetic compared to Ben and J.Lo's [actors Ben Affleck and Jennifer Lopez].

I can't present myself as a model of sexual self-acceptance. My postbaby, lapsed-gym-membership body image could use a boost. But I do know what feels good, and it rocks to have someone with whom I'm so comfortable, with whom there's very un-*Bachelorette*-like trust and history. It saddens me that in all the sex talk surrounding us, there's so little shout-out given to sex in a committed relationship. Last night was designated sex night for my husband and me (we have to schedule it, with a baby and killer work hours—otherwise we'd fall asleep watching *Trading Spaces* reruns), but before we got things rolling, we met in the upstairs bathroom. Jonathan started to cut his fingernails. As I watched the clippings plink into the sink, I said, "Dude, that is *so* not sexy." He looked at me and said, "Um, you should talk. You're holding the kitty litter scoop." Which had poop in it. I was not aware that I was cleaning out the cat's box as I was talking to him. And then we laughed, retired to bed and had tender, giggly sex; afterward, we held each other and told stories about the baby.

It's not glam. But it's authentic. And what the heck—I'm willing to talk about it. Maybe complete sexual comfort is a work in progress for every generation. I'm grateful to the women who talked to Kinsey about their own real, unmediated, nonairbrushed sex lives. Thanks to them, women today know to seek treatment for sexual dysfunction. Thanks to them, lesbians and bisexual women know they're far from alone. Thanks to them, we can buy pink Hello Kitty vibrators. (OK, maybe that last one's a reach, but the fact that we have sex toys aimed at *us* rather than at men is pretty cool.) If the trade-off for sex being out in the open is a glut of sexual imagery, hey, I'll take it. Because for people who'd otherwise be imprisoned by shame, knowing that there's a diverse sexual world out there is worth the advent of *Girls Gone Wild*—and maybe even the specter of men having intercourse with dessert.

"Most sexual taboos have evaporated. No matter how dark your thoughts, how unethical your desires, how absurd your fetish, everything is normal."

Sexual Freedom Has Gone Too Far

Ziauddin Sardar

Society's ideas about sex have changed so radically that almost any kind of sexual behavior is now considered normal, writes Ziauddin Sardar in the following viewpoint. Sexual gratification with the aid of pills, devices, and new computer technologies are increasingly available, yet few people seem concerned about how this preoccupation with sexual pleasure affects attitudes about loving relationships. The focus on sex as an end in itself rather than sex as an expression of intimate love is tragically self-centered, the author concludes. Sardar is the editor of *Futures*, a monthly journal.

As you read, consider the following questions:

1. According to the author, which age group is having the most sex?
2. What are the two remaining sexual taboos, in Sardar's opinion?
3. What "bewildering array of sexual orientations" is now being normalized, according to Sardar?

Ziauddin Sardar, "It's Just Mechanics; Viagra Is Just the Start: We'll Soon Have Pills That Make You Feel Deep Love and Video Games That Give Vibrations," *New Statesman*, vol. 134, January 1, 2005, pp. 30–33. Copyright © 2005 by New Statesman, Ltd. Reproduced by permission.

Is your sex life normal? The question was raised recently on the *Oprah Winfrey Show*. Tell us, the show asked its 20 million viewers, what turns you on, what turns you off, and what makes good sex.

The problem with such questions is that there are no "normal" answers. The normal is problematic because our ideas about sex have changed fundamentally. What constitutes normal is constantly refurbished. Its boundaries shift rapidly, and continue to shift. So what was abnormal yesterday—say, pornography—becomes normal today. And what is shunned today (say paedophilia) may just as easily become normal tomorrow.

Redefining Normal

One huge jump was provided by Viagra. In less than six years since the impotence pill came on the market, Viagra and its competitors, Levitra and Cialis, have transformed sexual norms and practices. As Meika Loe argues in *The Rise of Viagra*, it has redefined the concept of normal and changed the language of sex.

From the beginning, this was a treatment branded and marketed as normal. Impotence was called "erectile dysfunction", or simply ED—a common condition, as the football legend Pele assured us in TV ads, but not normal. Moreover, it did not arise from psychological causes or physical damage; rather, it was a simple medical condition rectified by a pill. Suddenly, drug company surveys discovered that more than half the US adult male population suffered from ED; figures for Europe were not far behind.

So if you can't get it up because you're pissed, stressed out, simply not in the mood or no longer find your partner attractive, you are actually suffering from a disease. And like all diseases, it must be cured. The cure is to swallow a pill and have sex no matter what, anywhere, any time, whenever. This has now become the norm.

Viagra is another step in stripping sex of all its complexity. Sex has been reduced to a simple question: for men, "how big?"; for women, "how long?". Combine these conundrums with other features of a market economy, such as availability on demand, choice, flexibility to mix'n'match, and we have new definitions not just of sex and love but of what it means to be human.

The "Silver Singles"

Today, to be normal, humans have sex right up to their last breath. It's the way to go. Sex is no longer the indulgence of the young. Nowadays, it is people over 50 who are having the most sex. With demographic shifts, high divorce rates and early retirement, the erstwhile golden generation of Sixties swingers who let it all hang out are now the "silver singles" (as they are called in America). The preoccupations of their youth have been sustained through their later years by medical enhancements. The wet dreams of 60-year-olds, who turned on to chemical enhancement in the Sixties, are a manifest example of future normality for us all.

What Viagra actually treats is loss of male power. In a confusing, depersonalising world busy reassigning status, regendering the social order, manipulating the ever-increasing demands of a commodified existence, sexual potency is the last bastion. Men, who have lost status and power almost everywhere, from workplace to home, must repair to the bedroom. Only there can they find the redemption of their true nature.

Sex and Love on Demand

However, in an age of sexual equality, men cannot be left alone with their predicament. The other half of humanity, too, finds it is not exempt from malfunction. Just a few months ago, the disease "female sexual dysfunction" hit the headlines. But female sexuality being what it is, women probably need something more than a pill. Simple enhanced blood flow, as laboratory tests have shown, is not good enough. So a female Viagra won't do the job as well as a vibrator or a dildo—soon to be widely and cheaply available from a Boots near you. A vibrator outperforms even a man on Viagra.

More serious aids to female performance are in the pipeline. In the next few years, patches and drugs to enhance vaginal lubrication and sensitivity will become available. A US surgeon has already patented a pacemaker-sized device which, implanted under the skin, triggers an orgasm. [In November 2004], clinical trials for the device were approved by the US Food and Drug Administration. Within a decade, it will be normal for every woman to have a perpetual orgasm whenever she wants it, wherever she needs it.

Love, too, will be available on demand. Recent research on love suggests that it consists of three basic biochemical elements. First, testosterone—which produces lust. Second, a group of amphetamine-like chemicals (dopamine, noradrenaline and phenylethylamine) produces feelings of euphoria that lead to infatuation. Third, if a relationship survives the first two rushes, a new biochemical response emerges, based on oxytocin, vasopressin and endorphins. This produces feelings of intimacy, trust and affection. Pharmaceutical companies are currently working on this third phase. So a "love pill" that modulates your subtler emotions and takes you straight to deep feelings of intimacy, trust and affection is just over the horizon. Science will fulfil the fairy tale. It will come up with a genuine love potion.

No More Sexual Taboos

The sexual liberation of every woman and man approaches its apotheosis: availability on demand with peak performance, assured gratification and enduring emotion. But much more has been let out of the bottle. The physical and psychological barriers to sex, identified as the ultimate metaphor for all the ills of humanity, had to be overcome. The consequence is that most sexual taboos have evaporated. No matter how dark your thoughts, how unethical your desires, how absurd your fetish, everything is normal. Your desire to dress up as a stuffed toy, your dreams of having sex with obese or dead people, your obsession with plastic or rubber, your fixation with asphyxiation—all that is sexually driven is OK.

Pornography's status as a taboo is rapidly disappearing. It has become part of the mainstream of western culture. Ancient Egyptians, Greeks and Romans had their erotica as esoterica on scrolls, pottery and frescos. Hindus have their erotic sculptures on temples. But in western culture pornography in unparalleled quantities and forms is communicated in every mass medium. Never before in history has there been so much pornography to be had by so many in such numerous ways.

Everyone is now just a click away from explicit, hard-core material. It is impossible to miss pornography on the internet because it seeks you out persistently, unannounced, at every opportunity. It is there on . . . innumerable digital channels every night.

Rogers. © 1998 by the *Pittsburgh Post-Gazette*. Reproduced by permission.

On MTV's reality show *The Real World*, you can witness bisexual group sex. Explicit sex, including shots of erect penises, can be viewed on [the] revisionist western drama *Deadwood*. Michael Winterbottom's *9 Songs*, which will go on general release shortly, offers a stream of close-ups of intercourse, fellatio, ejaculation and cunnilingus. The French art-house director Catherine Breillat has pioneered the transfer of porn stars into mainstream cinema. Her . . . film, *Anatomy of Hell*, is as graphic as it is bizarre. And if that doesn't satisfy you, you can go to a new breed of "pornaoke bars", just opened in Edinburgh [Scotland], where you can groan and grind karaoke-style to porno tapes.

When pornography becomes normal, where will we go next?

There are only two taboos left: sex with children, and incest. Attempts to "normalise" paedophilia have begun. A thesis by Richard Yuill, awarded a PhD by Glasgow University in December 2004, suggests that sex between adults and minors is a good and positive thing. Yuill's research, based on interviews with paedophiles and their victims, "challenges the assumption" that paedophiles are inherently abusive. It is only a matter of time before other academics start arguing that incest, too, is decent and wholesome. Graphic art films and television documentaries will follow. The organisations campaigning for the rights of paedophiles will have their case for "normality" made for them.

They may then be able to take their place among the bewildering array of sexual orientations already being normalised. Once upon a time, there were heterosexuals and the love that dared not speak its name. Gay men and lesbians have long since lost their reticence. Then bisexuals, transsexuals and the "kinky" found their identity. Now we have intersexuals and the polyamorous. A few months ago, *New Scientist* announced the discovery, in breathless prose, of asexuals. These folk don't like to have sex—horror of horrors—with anybody. There are even orientations within orientations. So we have such self-definition as non-op transsexual, TG butch, femme queen, gender-queer, cross-dresser, third gender, drag king or queen and transboy. In one recent episode of . . . *CSI: Crime Scene Investigation*, a murder victim was said to be part of a community of "plushies", people who enjoy sex while dressed up as stuffed animals.

Body-Mod and Virtual Sex

It is now normal to have your breasts removed or added to, have new genitals constructed, or sprinkle a dash of hormones for the appropriate, desired effect. Things are about to become even more complex. Within a decade or so, you will be able to modify your body almost totally, as you wish. You will be able to turn off all physical signs of gender, switch off the hormones and get rid of all secondary sexual characteristics. Then you can add on the bits you wish and "sculpt" your body in any shape you like. When gene therapy becomes common, things will be even easier. Already, there are people who are experimenting with this; and a "body-mod" subculture is thriving on the internet.

What you can't do in reality will soon be available in simulation. The emerging technology of haptics, or the telecommunication of sensation using a computer interface, will enable you to live your most horrific dreams in virtual reality. Haptic technologies simulate physical sensation of real objects and feed them to the user. The first generation of haptic technology can be experienced in certain video games for the Sony PlayStation where the joystick is used to simulate vibrations. The next generation, on its way from Rutgers University, will simulate pressure, texture and heat. Combine this with state-of-the-art graphics and some innovative software and you have a complete pornographic universe. As Eric Garland points out in the December 2004 issue of the American magazine *The Futurist*, among its first uses could be "pornography involving children and featuring violence". But what's the harm, as it is only a digitised child?

A Decline in Real Sex

Am I the only person to wonder if the constant shifting of the boundaries of the normal, while increasing our obsession with sex, has really improved our sex lives? On the contrary, I would argue, it has led to a decline in real sex. Genuine intimacy cannot be generated through a pill. Neither can sincere, unconditional love be simulated. When sex is reduced to mechanics and endurance, there is little to differentiate it from plumbing and maintenance. When gender becomes meaningless, sex becomes empty. When sexual choice becomes an end in itself, then the end is destined to be tragic.

Sex used to be intercourse because it was part of a context, a loving relationship. When sex is just sex, without any context, what good does it do you? That is the crux of the problem. It becomes the ultimate narcissism, the sole gratification of self-love.

Welcome to the masturbatory society.

"Human beings should have the right to express their sexual desires and enter into relationships as they see fit, as long as they do not harm others."

Sexual Freedom Should Be Embraced

Vern L. Bullough

People should have the right to enjoy sexual pleasure as long as they are being ethically responsible, writes Vern L. Bullough in the following viewpoint. He maintains that a free society should abandon taboos on premarital sex, homosexuality, transgenderism, pornography, and masturbation, and promote a more informed view of sexuality as both a source of pleasure and an expression of intimacy. Freely expressed sexuality that is nonexploitative and that is accompanied by care and concern for others should be embraced as part of a balanced and healthy life, Bullough contends. Bullough is an emeritus professor at the State University of New York.

As you read, consider the following questions:

1. According to Bullough, what has helped to expand the boundaries of human sexual expression?
2. What attitudes about sexuality have been harmful to human relationships, in the author's opinion?
3. In Bullough's view, what is fundamental in any sexual encounter or relationship?

Vern L. Bullough, "Declaration of Sexual Rights and Responsibilities," *Free Inquiry*, vol. 24, August/September 2004, pp. 52–54. Copyright © 2004 by the Council for Democratic and Secular Humanism, Inc. Reproduced by permission.

S exuality has long been denied its proper place among other human activities. It has often been shrouded in mystery and surrounded by taboos, or heralded far beyond its capacity to, by itself, contribute to the fullness of life. Clearly, human sexuality grows increasingly satisfying as life itself becomes more meaningful. This importance of sexuality can be illustrated by looking at its contributions to enhancing the quality of today's lifestyle.

For the first time in history, if proper precautions are taken, there need be very little fear of unwanted pregnancy or illness from a sexually transmitted disease. It is important that we recognize the changing role of sexuality which this change has brought about.

In the past, the legal limitations to conjugal unions or monogamous marriage were part of a social system in which reproduction was largely a matter of chance—and women were subject to men. Though a viable marriage has long been a cherished human relationship and will, we believe, continue to be, other types of sexual relationships have also been significant and need to be recognized. We believe that human beings should have the right to express their sexual desires and enter into relationships as they see fit, as long as they do not harm others or interfere with those others' right to sexual expression. This growing sense of sexual freedom, however, should be accompanied by a sense of ethical responsibility. That is the purpose of this "Bill of Sexual Rights and Responsibilities."

Expanding Sexual Boundaries

1. We believe the boundaries of human sexuality need to be expanded. Sex is more than procreation, and, though procreation will always be important, it is only one aspect of human sexual expression today. Alternative sexual activity has often been condemned in the past, but, in today's world, the widespread use of effective contraceptives as well as other developments in reproductive technology have made effective family planning possible for larger and larger numbers of people in the world. As a result, it is time that sexuality should be viewed as an expression of intimacy, a source of enjoyment and enrichment, and even a means for releasing tension. Sex should be integrated with other aspects of experience that are part of a balanced life.

2. *Developing a sense of equity between the sexes is an essential feature of a sensible morality.* All legal, occupational, economic, and political discrimination against women should be removed and all traces of historical sexism erased. Until women have equal opportunities, they will be vulnerable to continued exploitation by men. This means that men must recognize the right of women to control their own bodies and to determine the nature of their own sexual expression. All individuals—female or male—are entitled to equal consideration as persons.

Rejecting Harmful Taboos

3. *Repressive taboos should be replaced by a more balanced and objective view of sexuality based upon a sensitive awareness of human behavior and needs.* Archaic taboos have limited our thinking in many ways. The human person, especially the female, has often been held in bondage by restrictions that prescribed when, where, with whom, and with what parts of the body the sexual impulse could be satisfied. As these taboos are discarded, an objective reappraisal is required, although even without any formal authorization, changes have been taking place. Premarital sexual intercourse is being seen in a different light, and forced marriages are disappearing. Some individuals have multiple sexual relations, and organizations have appeared advocating polyamorous relationships. Homosexual relationships have finally been recognized as legal. Different lifestyles should also be permissible, including those engaged in by transvestites, transsexuals, and other transgendered or bisexual individuals. The guiding principles should be age and consent and how the activity affects others. On the whole, the use of genital associations to express feelings of genuine intimacy, rather than as simply connections for physical pleasure or procreation alone, is an important step forward.

Past taboos have prevented adequate examination of certain topics, thus blocking the discovery of answers to important questions associated with sexual activities. Abortion is a case in point. By focusing only on the destruction of the fetus, many have avoided facing the other issues that are fundamental, such as a woman's right to choose to be pregnant and the need to medically protect the mother.

There must be open discussion of ways of providing a comprehensive sex education for both children and adults. Adequate and accurate information about contraceptive procedures should be available to those who wish to use them or as something they might use in a special situation. Likewise, taboos that cause people to feel that viewing the genitals or seeing sexual intercourse is obscene and pornographic should be challenged. Sex must be treated as part of the natural experience of being human. And masturbation is one of the joys of sex and should be regarded as part of the natural experience of being human.

Facing Challenging Conditions

4. Each person has both an obligation and a right to be informed about the various civic and community aspects of human sexuality. A necessary first step is to affirm and support the statement of the United Nations World Health Organization's committee on human sexuality that every "person has the right to receive sexual information and to consider accepting sexuality for pleasure as well as for procreation." Even children have a right to sex education that is adjusted to their levels of understanding.

It is important to recognize that sexual attitudes are often intimately related to many problems of public importance, although taboos too often inhibit free discussion. For example, to deal effectively with extremely rapid population growth in different areas of the world we must accept that individual attitudes influence sexual expression and contraception choices. This requires research and experimentation. So does satisfying the sexual needs of individuals who are incarcerated or institutionalized for one reason or another and who still need to establish meaningful ties with others, whether they be in homes for senior citizens, for the developmentally disabled or mentally compromised, or in prison. In sum, sexual attitudes and lifestyles continually need to be adjusted to meet changing conditions brought on by technological and medical developments as well as changing cultural patterns. We often do not know the answers to these new problems, but we must recognize the need and deal with the reality.

Women and Sexual Freedom

Until relatively recently, women in the mainstream society did not always conduct sex or family lives on their own terms. Rather, because they lacked power, they were dependent on male authorities such as husbands, clergy, psychologists, and doctors, who prescribed and proscribed their proper places, often within a submissive and self-sacrificing female framework. These men, previously as women's only sources of official knowledge, enforced their own sexual agendas, telling women only what they thought they needed to know. But for the past four decades, various interconnected social forces have converged to give more women more authority over their own lives and to create and propel the sexual evolution. . . .

Feminists of the 1960s and 1970s had a powerful impact on future generations of women's being able to conduct their sex lives "her way." They redefined sex and sexual freedom from a woman's point of view, broadened women's knowledge of their own bodies, secured reproductive rights, and began to expand freedoms for lesbians and minorities. With new rights in education and the workplace, women were able to become independent, by either remaining single or divorcing, and to better control every aspect of their sex lives.

Paula Kamen, *Her Way: Young Women Remake the Sexual Revolution*, 2000.

5. Potential parents have both the right and responsibility to plan the number and the time of the birth of their children, taking into account both social needs and their own desires. Family size and the decision to give birth is up to the individuals involved. This means that birth control and abortion information as well as that about voluntary sterilization must be freely available to both married couples and unmarried individuals. Males as well as females should be involved in family planning decisions. Contraception should not be the sole responsibility of females. There is a need to urge more intensive research on an effective male contraceptive.

6. Sexual morality should come from a sense of caring and respect for others. Much of it cannot be legislated. Laws can and do protect the young from exploitation and people of any age from sexual abuse such as rape. And child sexual abuse is a major problem that must be given a high priority for serious research. But, beyond laws emphasizing the importance of age and consent, most forms of sexual expression should not be matters of legal regulation. Mature individuals should be able to choose their partners and the kinds of sexual expression suited to them.

Certain forms of sexual expression, such as being a prostitute or utilizing one, are regarded as demeaning or confining by many, but any changes in such practices should come through education and counseling and not by legal prohibition, although the conditions and locations of soliciting can be subject to regulation if they appear to endanger children or seriously violate the rights of others. The overriding objective should be to help individuals to live balanced and self-actualized lives. The punishment and ostracism of those who voluntarily engage in socially disapproved forms of sexual conduct only exacerbate the problem. Sexual morality should be viewed as an inseparable part of general morality —not as a special set of rules. Sexual values and sex acts, like other human values and acts, should be evaluated by whether they frustrate or enhance human fulfillment and avoid force and exploitation.

Individuals should not knowingly pass on a sexually transmitted disease. Such an action is harmful to another. Those who are diagnosed with a sexually transmitted disease should not be ostracized but should be treated as any other ill or diseased person.

7. *Physical pleasure has worth as a moral value.* Traditional religious and social views have often condemned pleasures of the body as "sinful," "wicked," or as major causes of illness. These attitudes are highly judgmental and very destructive of human relationships. Deprivation of physical pleasure, particularly during the formative periods of development, can and often does result in family breakdown, child abuse, adolescent runaways, alcoholism, and various forms of dehumanizing behavior. Physical pleasure within the context of meaningful human relationships is essential—both as a moral value and as a contribution to wholesome social relationships.

Sex and the Stages of Life

8. The ability of individuals to respond positively and affirmatively to sexuality throughout the life cycle must be acknowledged and accepted. These responses differ with the ages of individuals. Childhood sexuality is expressed through genital awareness and exploration, which involves self-touching or caressing parts of the body, behavior for which children should not be punished. It is a natural part of childhood and such learning experiences help the individual understand his or her body feelings and incorporate sexuality as an integral part of his or her personality. Masturbation is a viable mode of satisfaction for many individuals, both young and old, and should be fully accepted as part of being human. Just as repressive attitudes have prevented us from recognizing the importance of childhood sexual exploration, they can also prevent us from seeing the value of sexuality in the middle and later years of life. We need to appreciate the fact that older persons have sexual needs just as those much younger do. The joy of touching, of giving and receiving affection and the satisfaction of intimate body responsiveness is the right of everyone throughout life.

Healthy Expression

9. In all sexual encounters, commitment to human and humanistic values should always be present. No person's sexual desires should hurt or disadvantage another without their willing consent. This principle should apply to all sexual encounters—both to the brief and casual experience and to those that are deeper and more prolonged. In any sexual encounter or relationship, freely given consent is fundamental—even in the marital relationship.

These concepts raise troublesome and perplexing questions since those directly engaged in the encounter may hold widely differing points of view toward sexual conduct. This makes it essential that open, candid, and honest communication about current and future expectations takes place. Even then, decisions are subject to judgment and projection, and their outcomes are only slowly revealed.

No relationship, sexual or otherwise, occurs in a vacuum. In addition to the persons directly involved in the sexual relationship, there are important others—parents, children, siblings, friends, and other lovers or mates. The interest of these persons are usually complex and diverse, and no course of action will satisfy everyone. Even willing consent, however, is not enough to justify maiming or killing a person for the purpose of sexual satisfaction. The key is to have empathy for others. It is important to ask oneself, "How would I want others to conduct themselves sexually toward me and others that I care about?" Equally important to consider: "Am I concerned for the happiness and well-being of my partner or others involved or just for my own?" Each person contributes to creating a social atmosphere in which a full acceptance of responsible sexual expression should exist.

Freedom and Responsibility

The realization and acceptance of the points in this statement depend upon each individual recognizing that one has autonomy and control over one's own sexual function. Each individual needs to realize that it is reasonable to accept and enjoy pleasures of the body (and mind) and to respect the rights of others who also accept them.

At this point in our history, we human beings are embarking on a wondrous adventure. For the first time, we realize that we own our own bodies. Until now, our bodies have been in bondage to church or state, which have dictated how we could express our sexuality. Most people in the past have not been permitted to experience the pleasures and joys of the human body and their sensory nature to their fullest capacity. To do so, we need to accept the belief that actualizing pleasure is among the highest moral goods—so long as it is experienced with responsibility and mutuality and does not involve unwanted force or exploitation.

A reciprocal and creative attitude toward sexuality can have a deep meaning both for the individual and for society. Each of us will know its personal meaning, but we also need to experience it with others. In effect, our behavior can say to another, "I am enriched for having had this experience and for having contributed to your having had it also." The social meaning can derive from the loving feelings engendered in a person who is experiencing guilt-free, reciprocal pleasure. The loving feelings of mental and physical well-being, the sense of completion of the self that we can experience from freely expressed sexuality may well reach out to all humanity. It is quite impossible to have a meaningful, ecstatic sexual and sensual life and to be indifferent to or uncaring about other human beings.

Freeing our sexual selves is vital if we are to reach the heights of our full humanity. But at the same time, we believe that we need to activate and nourish a sense of our responsibilities to others.

"If marriage is redefined out of existence, our entire society will be harmed."

Same-Sex Marriage Will Undermine the Institution of Marriage

Robert P. George and David L. Tubbs

In the following viewpoint Robert P. George and David L. Tubbs maintain that federal legalization of same-sex marriage would distort human sexuality and seriously destabilize the institution of marriage. According to these authors, the majority of same-sex couples do not believe that monogamy is required in a committed relationship. The marriage of homosexuals, then, would mean that sexual fidelity and procreation no longer define the marital relationship. Redefining marriage to this extent will ultimately destroy it, the authors conclude. George, a professor at Princeton University, is the author of *In Defense of Natural Law* and a member of the President's Council on Bioethics. Tubbs is a political analyst at the American Enterprise Institute.

As you read, consider the following questions:

1. According to a University of Chicago study cited by George and Tubbs, what percentage of American men and women are sexually faithful in their marriages?
2. According to a 1999 survey of same-sex couples cited by the authors, what percentage of men and what percentage of women believed that a committed relationship entailed monogamy?
3. In the authors' opinion, who will be hurt the most by a redefinition of marriage?

Robert P. George and David L. Tubbs, "Redefining Marriage Away," *City Journal*, vol. 14, Summer 2004, pp. 26–28. Copyright © 2004 by the Manhattan Institute for Policy Research. Reproduced by permission.

C onservative advocates of same-sex marriage insist that their goal is not a radical alteration of the institution itself. They favor the legal recognition of same-sex partnerships as marriages in order to secure "equal rights," they say. Their goal in redefining marriage is not to weaken or abolish it but to expand access to it, while leaving its core features intact. Far from harming marriage, they contend, the move to same-sex marriage would strengthen the institution.

Though this argument has a certain superficial appeal, it is profoundly mistaken. The issue is not one of equality or the right to participate in a valuable social institution. What divides defenders of traditional marriage from those who would redefine it is a disagreement about the nature of the institution itself. Redefining marriage will, of course, fundamentally change the posture of law and public policy toward the meaning and significance of human sexuality, procreation, and the bond between the sexes. Even more important, there are powerful reasons to fear that the proposed redefinition of marriage will destabilize and undermine this already battered institution.

A Shocking Proposal

To understand the destabilizing effects, consider this scenario. A young man and woman are engaged to be married. A month before the wedding, the man approaches his fiancée to ask whether she will consider an "open marriage," in which they will free each other from the duty to be sexually faithful.

Even today, the man's proposal is shocking, and his bride-to-be will almost surely be horrified by it. Nearly everyone would say that what the man has proposed is something other than a true marriage, since the norm of sexual exclusivity within marriage is essential to the institution. That is why the overwhelming majority of couples entering marriage do not even discuss whether they will follow the norm; they simply accept it.

Do most American husbands and wives honor the principle of sexual exclusivity in practice? The best evidence says yes. In their rigorous and acclaimed 1994 study on American sexual behavior, University of Chicago sociologist Edward

Laumann and his associates found that 65 to 85 percent of American men and more than 80 percent of American women (in every age group) had no sex partners other than their spouses while married. These figures are remarkable, especially if we recall the many ways in which popular culture has mocked or trivialized human sexuality and the demands of marriage in recent decades.

Rejecting Sexual Exclusivity

But do most same-sex couples accept the norm of sexual exclusivity? In a 1999 survey of such couples in Massachusetts, sociologist Gretchen Stiers found that only 10 percent of the men and 32 percent of the women thought that a "committed" intimate relationship entailed sexual exclusivity. An essay called "Queer Liberalism?" in the June 2000 *American Political Science Review* reviewed six books that discussed same-sex marriage. None of the six authors affirmed sexual exclusivity as a precondition of same-sex marriage, and most rejected the idea that sexual fidelity should be expected of "married" homosexual partners. For more than a decade, a wide array of authors who favor redefining marriage to include same-sex partners have advanced similar views. In a 1996 essay in the *Michigan Law Review*, University of Michigan law professor David Chambers even suggested that marriage should be redefined to include sexual unions of three or more people—so-called polyamorous relationships.

Honest activists admit this widespread rejection of exclusivity. Writing in 1997, journalist and activist Michelangelo Signorile used the terms "postmodern" monogamy and "emotional" monogamy to describe the living arrangements of many same-sex couples. As those adjectives suggest, such arrangements do not entail sexual exclusivity as a matter of principle. Signorile also noted that "a great many gay men" simply favor "open" partnerships.

While Signorile was describing "monogamy with a little breathing room," activists in the organization known as Sex Panic took a more radical line, ridiculing the aspiration to monogamy and other "small-town values." Sex Panic was largely composed of academic "queer theorists" (men as well as women), and according to journalist Caleb Crain, it defended "bathhouses, promiscuity, and anonymous sex" from "moralizing forces." More recently, Andrew Sullivan, a supposedly conservative advocate of same-sex marriage, has praised the alleged "spiritual value" of anonymous sex.

What Homosexual Activists Seek

Homosexual activists like Rep. Barney Frank (D-Mass.) often ask, "How would giving me and my partner 'marriage' status hurt your marriage?"

Well, let's count the ways.

Marriage is the union of a man and a woman, not just the union of any two people. It binds two families, and forms kinship patterns that pass on family names and property. It provides the optimal home for raising children. Homosexual relationships do not expand the family tree. Instead, they form a lifeless, withered branch.

Creating a "counterfeit marriage" cheapens the real thing and undermines support in law and culture. Americans need to understand that this is *precisely* what homosexual activists seek.

Robert Knight, *Family Voice*, January/February 2004.

To outsiders, these views might be incomprehensible. Since the onset of AIDS, same-sex male couples would seemingly have an especially great incentive to embrace the norm of sexual exclusivity. The general unwillingness to do so is telling. Equally telling are accounts of rampant promiscuity among active male homosexuals before the AIDS epidemic, such as that provided by Randy Shilts in his 1987 best-seller *And the Band Played On.*

Same-Sex Marriages Will Be Unstable

Some proponents of same-sex marriage believe that its legalization will help same-sex partners be sexually faithful. The evidence, however, suggests that acceptance of the norm of sexual exclusivity is a minority view among homosexuals in the United States and elsewhere. Furthermore, because intimate relations between persons of the same sex are inherently —and not merely contingently—unconnected to procreation, there is no principled reason to limit same-sex marriage to two persons. Thus, one can reasonably predict that same-sex marriage is going to be intrinsically unstable, as Sex Panic recognized in expressing its contempt for the institution. As if to confirm these points, the first same-sex couple to receive a marriage license in Provincetown, Massachusetts, told the press that they had an "open" marriage.

By contrast, the norm of sexual exclusivity within real marriage is both intelligible and morally sound. The norm originates in the sexual complementarity of a husband and wife as a biological unit, and it functions to increase the likelihood that children will be reared by their biological parents. The norm binds a man and a woman in a covenant of mutual support, premised on the duties of fidelity and exclusivity. The norm is also meant to reduce vulnerability—not only of children but also of mothers and pregnant women.

In response, some might take the line of Yale law professor William Eskridge, who asserts that traditional marriage is now more "relational" rather than "procreational." But this view is wrong. In the past century, roughly 90 percent of American women were married by the age of 30, and between 80 and 90 percent had at least one child by the age of 40.

For all these reasons, the legal recognition of same-sex partnerships as "marriages" is likely to destabilize further an institution already damaged by the casual acceptance of cohabitation and unwed childbearing, as well as by the high rate of divorce. If a desire to stamp social approval on homosexual conduct and relationships leads to a redefinition of marriage that detaches it not only from biological complementarity and procreation but also from the related norm of sexual exclusivity, what will be left of the institution?

It is often remarked that marriage tends to "civilize" sexuality—particularly male sexuality. Although the complete picture is more complex than that, there is truth in this remark. But there is no magic in a word. Redefining marriage means abolishing it and shifting the label to a new institution —one for which there are no grounds of principle for sexual exclusivity or monogamy. Thus redefined, marriage won't function to civilize anybody. If marriage is redefined out of existence, our entire society will be harmed, but the harm will be distributed unequally. In the libertine utopia of "sexual freedom," women and children will suffer the most.

"Gays and lesbians have had nothing to do with [the decline of heterosexual marriage]."

Same-Sex Marriage Does Not Threaten the Institution of Marriage

Cynthia Tucker

The movement for gay and lesbian marriage is not responsible for the troubled state of traditional marriage, argues syndicated columnist Cynthia Tucker in the following viewpoint. The decline in stable heterosexual marriages is largely the result of modern cultural forces, including the emergence of two-career households, individualism, and overly idealized notions about marriage, she maintains. Heterosexual marriage also has connections to deeply flawed traditions, such as ancient laws that granted men power over women. Rather than blaming advocates for gay unions, analysts should have an honest debate about the real reasons for the decline in marriage, contends Tucker.

As you read, consider the following questions:
1. What are the challenges that confront contemporary married couples, according to Tucker?
2. According to the author, what false premise about traditional marriage is fostered by conservative activists?
3. How does the stability of gay and lesbian unions compare with the stability of heterosexual unions, according to Tucker?

It wasn't even close. The U.S. Senate easily shut down debate [in July 2004] over a proposed constitutional amendment banning gay marriage.

Democrats were joined by a handful of Republicans—including Arizona's John McCain—who remember the cornerstone of conservatism: Government has no business regulating citizens' private lives. As McCain put it, the amendment "strikes me as antithetical in every way to the core philosophy of Republicans."

The State of Heterosexual Marriage

With that ugly business behind us, perhaps it will be possible now to have a legitimate discussion about the dire state of heterosexual marriage. People of goodwill—those of all faiths and those with none—ought to be able to dispense with the lies and illogic that have poisoned the debate so that we can concentrate on the changed cultural expectations that bedevil modern marriage.

The two-career couple; the wife who earns more than her husband; disagreements over religion, money and child-rearing; old-fashioned adultery and betrayal—those are the challenges that confront contemporary couples. Not to mention a destabilizing factor embedded in 21st-century romance—the idealized Hollywood marriage, which gives young couples a false premise on which to base a lifetime pledge. (As a divorcee, I know something about the dilemmas that doom so many heterosexual marriages.)

As commonplace as those problems are, you haven't heard much about them in the debate over "saving" traditional unions. Instead, narrow-minded preachers and pandering politicians have propagated a lot of foolish notions; among the most foolish is the idea of a connection between the faltering state of traditional marriage and the growing movement for gay rights. Jennifer Lopez, Britney Spears and Trista and Ryan—who married in a televised ceremony after she spent a few weeks culling him from a herd of unattached males on a so-called reality show—have contributed to the decline of heterosexual marriage. Gays and lesbians have had nothing to do with it.

Conservative activists have also fostered the false premise

that marriage has always been defined as a union between one man and one woman. Nonsense. During 100,000 years of history of homo sapiens, marriage has been a union between one man and as many women as he could afford. The Bible tells us that King Solomon had a thousand wives and concubines. If you've read the record of any ancient civilization—whether the history of the ancient Israelites or the history of the ancient Greeks—you know that women were considered property, first the property of their fathers, later of their husbands, to be treated as the men saw fit.

What Is Marriage About?

Marriage is about more than reproduction. It's also about companionship. It's about the socially stabilizing value of sexual monogamy. It's about the power of long-term, committed partnerships to achieve more in a variety of areas than individuals can on their own. . . .

I would no more deny gay people the right or opportunity to form such a union than I would deny an elderly or sterile heterosexual couple that right. They, too, can benefit from the solemnity and social recognition of permanent commitment. They, too, can find comfort and health in sanctioned monogamy. They, too, can use the solidity of a formalized, permanent relationship to do more and be more as individuals—to strengthen their communities, their workplaces, their social networks.

Eric Zorn, *Family in America*, August 2003.

In other words, there is a good reason that traditional marriage is in trouble. Many of those traditions were deeply flawed. If you don't understand the laws and traditions that have governed the treatment of women for thousands of years, you cannot possibly appreciate the ways in which cultural change has shaken the foundations of marriage.

Nor does the more traditional philosophy still preached by many conservative Christian churches—that the man should be the unquestioned head of his household—seem to make those unions stronger than others in which the man and woman share power. According to a study released [in 2001] by The Barna Research Group Ltd., "born-again Christians are just as likely to get divorced as non-born-again adults." And 90 percent of those divorces occurred "after they accepted Christ, not before."

(Gay and lesbian unions, by the way, encounter the same difficulties and evidence the same variety that heterosexual unions have shown. Some are loving and stable unions that last a lifetime. Many are not. How could it be otherwise, since gays are subject to the same cultural forces that affect the rest of us?)

The Need for Honest Debate

It may be that, in the broad sweep of human history, traditional marriage is doomed. As human beings live longer and longer lives, the idea that one partner can satisfy our desire for love, stability and happiness forever may come to seem quaint.

But I still believe in the institution of marriage, still believe it is worth saving. Whatever else it has been, it has functioned as a building block of civilization. And a loving and stable marriage remains, I believe, the best institution for bringing well-adjusted children into adulthood.

The institution deserves at least an honest debate. It hasn't gotten that. We cannot begin to work on restoring heterosexual marriage unless we are candid about the cultural changes—starting with the Enlightenment and its emphasis on the individual—that have contributed to its decline. This vicious and vulgar business of blaming gays and lesbians gets us nowhere.

Periodical Bibliography

The following articles have been selected to supplement the diverse views presented in this chapter.

Nina Bernstein	"Behind Fall in Pregnancy, a New Teenage Culture of Restraint," *New York Times*, March 7, 2004.
Vern L. Bullough	"Alfred Kinsey and the Kinsey Report: Historical Overview and Lasting Contributions," *Journal of Sex Research*, May 1998.
Benedict Carey	"Long After Kinsey, Only the Brave Study Sex," *New York Times*, November 9, 2004.
Bryce Christensen	"Why Homosexuals Want What Marriage Has Become," *Family in America*, April 2004.
Jeremiah Creedon	"Everything You Always Wanted to Know . . . ," *Utne Reader*, September/October 2003.
Benoit Denizet-Lewis	"Friends, Friends with Benefits, and the Benefits of the Local Mall," *New York Times Magazine*, May 30, 2004.
Anthony Esolen	"Our Peculiar Institution: The New Slavery," *Crisis: Politics, Culture, and the Church*, September 2004.
Mitchell Kalpakgian	"The Sexual Revolution Is Doomed," *New Oxford Review*, February 1999.
Jennifer Roback Morse	"Sex Fiction," *American Enterprise*, April/May 2005.
Judith Reisman	"Kinsey's Hidden Child Abuse," *New American*, December 13, 2004.
Roger Scruton	"Shameless and Loveless," *Spectator*, April 16, 2005.
Adam Tenney	"Whose Family Values?" *Political Affairs*, April 2004.
Karen Testerman	"Promiscuous Plague," *World & I*, March 2004.
Leonore Tiefer	"The Opposite of Sex," *Ms.*, August/September 1999.

CHAPTER 2

What Sexual Norms Should Society Uphold?

Chapter Preface

Cohabitation—the term generally used to describe the status of unmarried sexual partners who share a household—has become commonplace in much of the Western world. Once perceived as scandalous and immoral, cohabitation has increased by 1,000 percent in the United States since 1960, with more than 4.7 million couples currently living together and with 56 percent of all first marriages preceded by cohabitation. In the 1950s one in ten heterosexual American women chose to live with their partners before marriage; today one in three do so. In England today, 70 percent of single women live with their partners before marriage, compared to just 5 percent in the 1960s. And in Sweden, there are currently about two married couples for every cohabiting couple.

Many experts are disturbed by the prevalence of cohabitation because it seems to correspond with the increased rate of divorce over the past thirty years. One often-cited statistic—that cohabiting couples who marry have a 46 percent higher rate of divorce than noncohabitors who marry—disquiets researchers. Some analysts maintain that cohabiting couples are less committed to the notion of wedlock and therefore find it relatively easy to leave a troubled marriage. Others argue that cohabiting itself establishes a relationship pattern that emphasizes personal freedom over commitment—a pattern that is hard for couples to unlearn once they are married. Sociologist David Popenoe maintains that cohabitation may look like a progressive family trend on the surface but is, in the end, an enemy of marriage. "Marriage remains a cornerstone of a successful society," asserts Popenoe. "In place of more cohabitation, we should be trying harder to revitalize marriage. Particularly helpful in this regard would be educating young people about marriage from the early school years onward, teaching them how to make the wisest choices in their lifetime mates and stressing the importance of long-term marital commitment."

Most cohabiting couples, however, are grateful for the increased societal acceptance of their relationships. Some of these couples maintain that they have chosen to live together because they actually take wedding vows quite seriously and view cohabitation as a kind of "trial marriage" that lets them see if their relationship will last. As *Glamour* writer Robyn Brown writes,

> The only thing perfect about marriage is the airbrushed wedding photo. Living together helps you see past romanticized notions and clue in to what marriage will really be like. If my boyfriend and I ever decide to tie the knot, it will mean even more, because we'll both fully understand the vows we're taking. When they say "Do you promise to love, honor, and cherish," we'll know what they're really asking.

On the other hand, some committed couples see no need to ever exchange legal vows. "This is a marriage in heart and spirit," explains psychotherapist Amy Pine in describing her live-in relationship of fifteen years. "It's just that we didn't need to have it sanctioned by the government."

The great increase in the number of couples who live together outside of marriage suggests that cohabitation may establish itself as a norm in the Western world. In the following chapter analysts discuss the viability of cohabitation and other controversial proposals such as youth virginity pledges and gay marriage.

"The evidence concerning the positive effects of virginity pledges is extremely strong."

Virginity Pledges Benefit Youths

Robert Rector, Kirk A. Johnson, and Jennifer Marshall

The authors of the following viewpoint contend that teens who take formal pledges to remain virgins until marriage are less likely to have unprotected sex and to give birth out of wedlock. According to the National Longitudinal Study of Adolescent Health, virginity pledgers are less likely to be sexually active as teens, have fewer sexual partners than other youths, and consequently improve their chances of having healthy, stable lives. Robert Rector is senior research fellow in domestic policy, Kirk A. Johnson is senior policy analyst in the Center for Data Analysis, and Jennifer Marshall is director of domestic policy studies at the Heritage Foundation, a conservative think tank.

As you read, consider the following questions:

1. On average, how many sexual partners have non-pledgers had by the time they reach their early twenties, according to the authors? How many sexual partners have pledgers had?
2. According to the Add Health survey, what percentage of girls who take virginity pledges give birth before turning eighteen?
3. Why are some analysts skeptical about the impact of virginity pledge programs, according to the authors?

Robert Rector, Kirk A. Johnson, and Jennifer Marshall, "Teens Who Make Virginity Pledges Have Substantially Improved Life Outcomes," a publication of the Heritage Center for Data Analysis, www.heritage.com, September 21, 2004. Copyright © 2004 by The Heritage Foundation. Reproduced by permission.

Adolescents who take a virginity pledge have substantially lower levels of sexual activity and better life outcomes when compared with similar adolescents who do not make such a pledge, according to recently released data from the National Longitudinal Study of Adolescent Health (Add Health survey). Specifically, adolescents who make a virginity pledge:

- Are less likely to experience teen pregnancy;
- Are less likely to be sexually active while in high school and as young adults;
- Are less likely to give birth as teens or young adults;
- Are less likely to give birth out of wedlock;
- Are less likely to engage in risky unprotected sex; and
- Will have fewer sexual partners.

In addition, making a virginity pledge is not associated with any long-term negative outcomes. For example, teen pledgers who do become sexually active are not less likely to use contraception.

An Informative Study

Data from the National Longitudinal Study of Adolescent Health, which is funded by more than 17 federal agencies, show that the behavior of adolescents who have made a virginity pledge is significantly different from that of peers who have not made a pledge. Teenage girls who have taken a virginity pledge are one-third less likely to experience a pregnancy before age 18. Girls who are strong pledgers (defined as those who are consistent in reporting a virginity pledge in the succeeding waves of the Add Health survey) are more than 50 percent less likely to have a teen pregnancy than are non-pledgers.

Teens who make a virginity pledge are far less likely to be sexually active during high school years. Nearly two-thirds of teens who have never taken a pledge are sexually active before age 18; by contrast, only 30 percent of teens who consistently report having made a pledge become sexually active before age 18.

Teens who have made a virginity pledge have almost half as many lifetime sexual partners as non-pledgers have. By the time they reach their early twenties, non-pledgers have had, on average, six different sex partners; pledgers, by contrast, have had three.

Girls and Virginity Pledges

Girls who have taken a virginity pledge are one-third less likely to have an out-of-wedlock birth when compared with those who have never taken a pledge. Girls who are strong pledgers (those who are consistent in reporting a virginity pledge in the succeeding waves of the Add Health survey) are half as likely to have an out-of-wedlock birth as are non-pledgers.

Girls who make a virginity pledge also have fewer births overall (both marital and nonmarital) as teens and young adults than do girls who do not make pledges. By the time they reach their early twenties, some 27.2 percent of the young women who have never made a virginity pledge have given birth. By contrast, the overall birth rate of peers who have made a pledge is nearly one-third lower, at 19.8 percent.

Because they are less likely to be sexually active, pledging teens are less likely to engage in unprotected sex, especially unprotected nonmarital sex. For example, 28 percent of non-pledging youth reported engaging in unprotected non-marital sex during the past year, compared with 22 percent of all pledgers and 17 percent of strong pledgers. . . .

Overall, making a virginity pledge is strongly associated with a wide array of positive behaviors and outcomes while having no negative effects. The findings presented in this paper strongly suggest that virginity pledge and similar abstinence education programs have the potential to substantially reduce teen sexual activity, teen pregnancy, and out-of-wedlock childbearing.

True Love Waits

For more than a decade, organizations such as True Love Waits have encouraged young people to abstain from sexual activity. As part of these programs, young people are encouraged to take a verbal or written pledge to abstain from sex until marriage. In recent years, increased public policy attention has been focused on adolescents who take these "virginity pledges" as policymakers seek to assess the social and behavioral outcomes of such abstinence programs.

One major source of data on teens who have made virginity pledges is the National Longitudinal Study of Adolescent Health, funded by the Department of Health and Human Services and other federal agencies. The Add Health survey started with interviews of junior-high and high-school–aged students in 1994. In that year, and in subsequent interviews, adolescents were asked whether they had ever taken a virginity pledge. The students were tracked through high school and into early adulthood. By 2001, most of the youth in the survey were between the ages of 19 and 25—old enough to evaluate the relationship between pledging as teens and a variety of social outcomes.

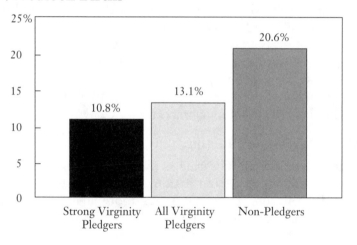

Percent of Women Who Have Out-of-Wedlock Births

National Longitudinal Study of Adolescent Health, 2004. www.cpc.unc.edu/projects/addhealth.

As noted, the Add Health survey is longitudinal, which means that it surveys the same group of adolescents repeatedly over time. Interviews were conducted in three succeeding years: Wave I in 1994, Wave II in 1995, and Wave III in 2001. In each of these years, individuals were asked the question: "Have you ever signed a pledge to abstain from sex until marriage?" We have grouped the Add Health youth into four categories based on their responses to this repeated question.

- *Non-pledgers.* These individuals answered that they had not taken a virginity pledge in each of the three waves of the survey.
- *Pledgers.* These individuals responded in at least one wave of the survey that they had made a virginity pledge.
- *Strong pledgers.* These individuals form a subset of the general pledger group; they affirmed in at least one wave of the survey that they had made a pledge and did not provide contradictory data in any subsequent wave. . . .
- *Weak pledgers.* These individuals form a second subset of the pledger group. These respondents reported in at least one wave of the survey that they had "ever taken a virginity pledge," but their responses were inconsistent; on a subsequent wave, they reported that they had not taken a pledge. Either these individuals ignored or forgot their previous response that they had made a pledge, or they interpreted the question differently in later years.

All adolescents were first placed in either the non-pledger or pledger category. All pledgers were subsequently placed in the weak or strong pledge categories. The four pledge categories are used throughout this paper to measure the behavioral correlates of pledging. . . .

Out-of-Wedlock Births

Out-of-wedlock childbearing is one of the most important social problems facing our nation. Children born and raised outside marriage are seven times more likely to live in poverty than are children born and raised in intact married families. Children born out of wedlock are five times more likely to be dependent on welfare when compared with those born and raised within wedlock. In addition, children born out of wedlock are more likely to become involved in crime, to have emotional and behavioral problems, to be physically abused, to fail in school, to abuse drugs, and to end up on welfare as adults.

The Add Health survey offers the good news that teenage girls who take a virginity pledge are:

- Substantially less likely to give birth in their teens or early twenties, and

• Less likely to give birth out of wedlock.

[The research shows that] girls who make a virginity pledge are less likely to give birth before their 18th birthday. Some 1.8 percent of the strong pledgers surveyed had given birth before 18; the rate for non-pledging girls was twice as high, at 3.8 percent.

By the time they reach their early twenties, non-pledging young women remain far more likely to have become pregnant and to have given birth than are peers who have made a pledge. [The data] shows that, by the time of the Wave III survey, some 27.2 percent of non-pledging girls had given birth to at least one child. By contrast, about one-third fewer (19.8 percent) of the girls who "had ever made a pledge" had given birth.

The contrast in out-of-wedlock childbearing is even stronger. As [the graph on page 65] shows, by Wave III of the survey in 2001, 20.6 percent of non-pledging girls had given birth out of wedlock. The rate of out-of-wedlock births among strong pledgers was nearly 50 percent lower, at 10.8 percent. . . .

Risky Sexual Behavior

Pledgers are significantly less likely than non-pledgers to engage in unprotected sexual activity (i.e., to have intercourse without contraception). While previous reports have suggested that sexually active pledgers are less likely to use contraception than non-pledgers are, examination of the Wave III data of the Add Health survey does not confirm this. In fact, as [the research] shows, pledgers who are sexually active are slightly more likely to use contraception than are their counterparts among the non-pledging group. However, the difference between the groups is not statistically significant.

Moreover, examination of sexually active youths presents only part of the picture. As noted previously, pledgers are far more likely to abstain from sexual activity entirely. Thus, when all youths (both those who are sexually active and those who are inactive) are examined, the data show that pledgers are substantially less likely to endanger themselves or others through unprotected sexual activity. As [the study] shows, 17.1 percent of strong pledgers reported having engaged in unprotected sex in the last survey year, compared to 28.2 percent of non-pledgers. Pledging is linked to a significant reduction in risky behavior. . . .

Two Clear Facts

The Add Health survey provides a wealth of important data about the sexual behavior of teens and young adults. These data reveal two clear facts about teens and virginity pledges.

• *Fact #1:* Teens who make virginity pledges have far better life outcomes and are far less likely to engage in risky sexual behavior when compared with teens who do not pledge. In general, teens who make virginity pledges are much less likely to become sexually active while in high school, to experience a teen pregnancy, and to have children out of wedlock. Compared with non-pledgers, teens who pledge have substantially fewer sex partners and are less likely to engage in unprotected sexual activity.

• *Fact #2:* The behavioral differences between pledging and non-pledging teens cannot be explained by differences in social background characteristics such as race, family income, and religiosity. Holding social factors constant, taking a virginity pledge is independently correlated with a broad array of positive behaviors and life outcomes.

Overall, the evidence concerning the positive effects of virginity pledges is extremely strong. Nevertheless, skeptics might argue that the simple fact that teens who make virginity pledges have substantially improved behaviors does not prove that virginity pledge programs themselves have a positive impact on behavior. It is conceivable that participating in a virginity pledge program and taking a pledge merely reinforce pro-abstinence decisions that the teen would have made without the program or pledge. From this perspective, virginity pledge programs may be a redundant "fifth wheel" that has no effect, rather than an operative factor leading to less risk-related behavior.

Given the limitations of the Add Health data, it is impossible to fully disprove this type of skepticism. Nonetheless, such an argument goes against common sense. Teens do not make decisions about sexual values in a vacuum. A decision to abstain and delay sexual activity does not emerge in a teen's mind *ex nihilo*, but rather will reflect the sexual values and messages that society communicates to the adolescent.

Promoting Abstinence Values

Regrettably, teens today live in a sex-saturated popular culture that celebrates casual sex at an early age. To practice abstinence, teens must resist pressure from peers and the media, in addition to controlling physical desire. It seems implausible to expect teens to abstain from sexual activity in the absence of social institutions (such as virginity pledge programs) that teach strong abstinence values. Similarly, it seems implausible that programs that teach clear abstinence values will have no influence on behavior, even among teens who embrace those values.

Since decisions to practice abstinence do not emerge in a vacuum, it seems very likely that the messages in virginity pledge programs contribute to positive behavior among youth. Participation in virginity pledge programs encourages youth to make pro-abstinence choices, and publicly taking an abstinence pledge reinforces teens' commitment to this decision and helps them to stick with the abstinence lifestyle.

The bottom line is simple: Teens who participate in virginity pledge programs and respond affirmatively to the messages in the program are far less likely to engage in risky behaviors and will have far better life outcomes than those who do not. Consequently, it would be best to expose teens to more, rather than fewer, pro-abstinence messages.

> *"[Attempts to promote virginity] ignore adolescents who initially heed the prevention messages but become sexually active later."*

Virginity Pledges Do Not Benefit Youths

J. Dennis Fortenberry

J. Dennis Fortenberry is a professor of pediatrics and medicine at the Indiana University Department of Medicine. In the following viewpoint he maintains that the promotion of adolescent virginity pledges can have adverse effects. According to data provided by the National Longitudinal Study of Adolescent Health, many teens who take the pledge eventually become sexually active and less likely to use condoms than are nonpledgers, which places them at risk for contracting sexually transmitted diseases. In addition, Fortenberry explains, pledgers are more likely to engage in unprotected oral and anal sex, practices that also carry an increased health risk. Fortenberry concludes that the abstinence-only message embodied in the virginity pledge does not adequately educate youths about sexual health.

As you read, consider the following questions:

1. Why is it important to recognize the difference between abstinence as a personal choice and the promotion of abstinence as a public health intervention, in Fortenberry's opinion?
2. What potential biases are embedded in the Add Health survey, according to Fortenberry?

J. Dennis Fortenberry, "The Limits of Abstinence-Only in Preventing Sexually Transmitted Infections," *Journal of Adolescent Health*, vol. 36, April 2005, pp. 269–70. Copyright © 2005 by the Society for Adolescent Medicine. Reproduced by permission.

O ver the past century, public health approaches to sexually transmitted infections (STIs) have come from 1 of
2 camps. Although specific policies certainly reflected the
times in which they arose, the debate over STI prevention
today is surprisingly similar to that of the early 20th century.
One camp advocates comprehensive education and skills.
The other focuses only on eliminating adolescent sexual activity. Today, national as well as state and local public health
policy is driven increasingly by an abstinence-only-until-
marriage prevention approach. Although supporters of this
approach to policy may have varied religious and moral
agendas, abstinence is promoted by them as unambiguous,
safe, and 100% effective. These claims are based on a common sense foundation of epidemiologic causality: sexual activity is a necessary and sufficient cause for infection transmission when 1 partner is infected.

Abstinence Policies Are Not Effective

However, despite traditional appeal and logical relevance,
public health policy based solely on abstinence has not been
shown to be effective. One deficiency of the abstinence-only
argument is its failure to distinguish between abstinence as a
personal choice and abstinence as a public health intervention. As a personal choice, abstinence is always 100% effective for STI prevention because, logically, abstinence cannot
simultaneously be nonabstinence. However, as a public
health intervention used at a population level, abstinence almost certainly will have a failure rate, even if it is successful
in a larger sense. For example, simulation studies suggest
that abstinence appears to be about as good as condoms for
the prevention of STI. Furthermore, potentially adverse effects of abstinence-only interventions have not been addressed systematically. The assumption that abstinence-only
interventions are without negative consequences has not
been tested in careful, longitudinal research.

The study by [Hannah] Brückner and [Peter] Bearman in
[the April 2005] issue of the *Journal of Adolescent Health* begins to address these issues. Data for the study were obtained
from the National Longitudinal Study of Adolescent Health
(Add Health). Methodologic details of the Add Health study

are described in detail in the article and are available publicly. The . . . article contains a methodologic innovation that deserves attention. Add Health respondents were asked on 3 different occasions whether they had ever taken a virginity pledge. Those who consistently reported never making a virginity pledge were classified as nonpledgers. Those who consistently reported making a virginity pledge were classified as consistent pledgers. Participants who reported making a pledge at some earlier date but subsequently reported never having made a virginity pledge were classified as inconsistent pledgers. This methodologic innovation is important because it allows us to examine pledging effects among adolescents who may be assumed to have different levels of commitment to pledging.

Many Pledgers Have Sex Before Marriage

An earlier analysis of Add Health data, replicated by Bearman and Brückner, showed that pledgers as a group become sexually active at older ages than nonpledgers. In fact, data in the [2005] article show that up to 25% of consistent pledgers report no lifetime sexual intercourse by age 25. The current data also suggest that consistent pledgers marry at younger ages than either nonpledgers or inconsistent pledgers. This suggests that pledgers are subject to lower levels of STI risk than nonpledgers. Brückner and Bearman do not address issues such as marital and sexual satisfaction, or marital stability of pledgers and nonpledgers, leaving open questions about other, perhaps unintended, effects. Married participants had fewer STIs than unmarried participants. However, infection rates among the married participants did not differ based on whether or not a virginity pledge was made during adolescence. From a public health perspective, marriage was a useful but imperfect protection against STIs among young adults, and adolescent virginity pledges did not enhance the STI protective effects of subsequent marriage.

Implicit in these data is the fact that a substantial proportion of adolescent virginity pledgers became sexually active outside of marriage. In fact, 88% of pledgers who reported sexual intercourse did so before marriage. In what may be Brückner's and Bearman's most important finding, STIs

The Limitations of "True Love Waits"

Because most adolescents eventually become sexually active during their teenage years, is it really wise to ban discussion of contraception and STD [sexually transmitted disease] protection from sex education? Although virtually all adolescents say they learned about STDs in school, other studies have shown that many adolescents underestimate their infection risk and that they have mistaken ideas about what protects them from STDs and what does not. The organizations that promote pledging and other abstinence-only programs have been hostile to programs that combine abstinence education with information about how to prevent pregnancy and STDs for sexually active adolescents. The materials distributed by "True Love Waits" and other organizations teach adolescents that the only protection from pregnancy and STDs is abstinence. The all-or-nothing approach advocated by many abstinence-only programs may create additional barriers to knowledge and protection for adolescents. For example, the emphasis on virginity may encourage adolescents to limit their sexual activity to noncoital behaviors, which may nevertheless expose them to risks of infection. In this context, it is important to know that pledgers are less likely than nonpledgers to be tested for STDs, and to have ever seen a doctor because they are worried about an STD. If STDs were more likely to go untreated among pledgers, higher STD prevalence may result even in the presence of lower incidence rates.

Hannah Brückner and Peter Bearman, *Journal of Adolescent Health*, April 2005.

---

among young adults did not significantly differ according to whether or not a virginity pledge was made at some point during adolescence. This is despite the fact that pledgers have fewer years of sexual exposure, fewer partners, and fewer risky partners. The STI protective effects of virginity pledges for adolescents, if any, have disappeared completely by young adulthood.

At Risk for Sexually Transmitted Diseases

The question of whether virginity pledges have short-term protective effects cannot be comparably addressed by the Add Health data because STI screening tests were obtained only when participants were young adults, not during their participation as adolescents. However, Brückner and Bearman do offer 3 additional findings of clinical and public health relevance. First, pledgers who became sexually active were less likely to use condoms at first sex than nonpledgers. Because a substantial proportion of pledgers did become sexually active, this increases concern about increased STI risk for these adolescents. Second, pledgers are more likely to engage in noncoital oral-genital and anogenital sexual behaviors that represent some risk for STI. Finally, pledgers were less likely to seek and obtain care related to STIs. This is an area that deserves additional research because of the importance of perceived risk and stigma in adolescents' STI-related care-seeking.

Are there potential biases or issues that suggest inferences other than those offered by the authors? Readers should note some additional issues. First, the data are not representative of all adolescents. Because the Add Health survey uses schools as its basic sampling frame, out-of-school adolescents—likely at higher risk for STIs than those in school—are unrepresented. If out-of-school adolescents were less likely to make virginity pledges, one might argue that the Add Health data underrepresents STI rates among nonpledgers.

Second, alternative explanations might be important if 1 of the 3 pledge groups were more or less likely to participate as young adults. Brückner and Bearman addressed this issue in some detail, with little evidence for significant influence on the results.

Finally, the results represent data from a survey, not an experiment. Because the pledge intervention was not assigned randomly to adolescents, the complex personal, family, religious, and sociocultural selectivity that may influence a decision to make a virginity pledge cannot be assessed fully. It is possible that making a virginity pledge is simply a marker for adolescents with specific characteristics associated with later onset of sexual activity in the first place.

Virginity Pledges Have a Limited Impact

Perhaps the most important lesson to take from these data is the confirmation that absolutist approaches to STI prevention, whatever their moral, religious, or philosophic origins, incompletely serve those at risk. The data suggest that the vivid national dialogue about the content of STI prevention messages for adolescents has helped create a social environment in which abstinence, until an older age or until marriage, is a relevant choice. However, abstinence-only prevention efforts such as those represented by virginity pledges clearly are limited. They lack effectiveness for a substantial proportion of teenagers who become sexually active during early adolescence. They ignore adolescents who initially heed the prevention messages but become sexually active later. In addition, they may, in fact, cause harm by decreasing perceived risk or increasing stigma. Sexuality is a complex developmental moving target that enriches lives as well as increases risk for adverse health consequences. From a public health perspective, we must get past notions that simple, perfectly effective, and completely harm-free interventions exist for any of the health-harming consequences of sexuality.

"Living together without marriage, once unheard of, has become commonplace in America today."

Cohabitation Is a Viable Lifestyle Choice

Dorian Solot and Marshall Miller

An increasing number of American couples are living together without being married, report Dorian Solot and Marshall Miller in the following viewpoint. Cohabitation is actually rather common, with many partners choosing to live together before marriage as well as those who remain in long-term commitments without ever getting married. The authors contend that cohabitation offers couples the chance to get to know one another better before marriage. Despite the growing acceptance of cohabitation, unmarried couples still face strong pressures to marry from society, families, and employers, Solot and Miller contend. The trend toward nontraditional family forms, however, will likely continue, they conclude. Solot and Miller are the founders of the Alternatives to Marriage Project, an organization that promotes equality for unmarried people.

As you read, consider the following questions:

1. About how many unmarried couples are there in the United States today, according to Solot and Miller?
2. What events provoked the authors to form the Alternatives to Marriage Project?
3. According to Solot and Miller, what is the most common kind of discrimination that cohabiting couples experience?

Duncan Smith remembers when, not so long ago, hotel check-in clerks requested evidence that he was married to his wife. Back then, he says, "If you wanted to be with someone, you had to be married."

Times have changed. Today, Smith, now divorced, lives with Lydia Breckon in the Edgewood neighborhood of Cranston, [Rhode Island], with their three dogs and a cat. For 11 years, they've shared their lives, their cooking and cleaning, and their vacations. People sometimes assume they are married. But they have never taken a trip down the aisle together.

They describe themselves as pragmatists, not radicals. "I don't have a banner or a flag. I don't march around saying [being unmarried] is the right way to live. But on the other hand, I feel totally comfortable," Breckon says.

A Common Choice

Living together without marriage, once unheard of, has become commonplace in America today. Parents often advise children to delay marriage and live with a partner to test the relationship, and growing numbers are forgoing marriage altogether. Unlike gay and lesbian couples, whose fight to legalize same-sex marriage has dominated recent headlines, those who choose not to marry receive little attention for their unique situation.

According to the US Census, 12,000 partners like Smith and Breckon live together in Rhode Island without being married. Nationally, there are 5.6 million, a fivefold increase since 1970. "Today, the *Ozzie and Harriet* family[1] only constitutes about 10 percent of all families. Family diversity is now the norm," says Los Angeles attorney Thomas Coleman, an expert on family diversity and marital status discrimination.

Coleman attributes the change to a list of factors, including women in the workforce, changing religious attitudes, no-fault divorce laws, and greater visibility of gay, lesbian, bisexual, and transgendered [GLBT] people. Yet many unmarried people say that government and private industry

---

1. *Ozzie and Harriet* was a television show of the 1950s and 1960s that featured a traditional two-parent family.

have been slow to keep up with the times by implementing laws and workplace policies that recognize the new structures of families.

Most cohabiting couples will marry eventually. For many, living together is a logical way to experience a relationship without making a lifelong commitment. Ken Heskestad of Providence says, "[Living together without marriage] makes me more conscious of what I have and makes me devote more of my energies to the relationship." Living together saves money as well, another common reason people decide to move in with a sweetheart.

Significant numbers of people, however, decide to stay together long-term without a formal exchange of "I do's." Their reasons vary. Some, like Jane Fronek, Heskestad's partner, say the choice not to marry allows her a freedom from assumed roles. "Once you are considered someone's wife, people treat you in a certain way, and that is something that really scares me," says Fronek.

Commitment Phobic?

Television talk shows label unmarried couples "commitment phobic," but many say that their level of commitment to a relationship has nothing to do with its legal status. In California, Amy Lesen's parents divorced when she was a child, and her father went on to have a successful 20-years-and-counting relationship without being married.

Today, Amy says she does not want to marry her partner. "I saw one marriage break up, and I saw two people who did not get married stay together for the rest of my life. I think that it drove a point home to me that [marriage] does not really matter," she says.

Some people find the institution of marriage too bound to religion. Some have experienced painful or expensive divorces and have sworn never to involve the legal system in their relationships again. Growing numbers of senior citizens find that they would lose a significant amount of the pension they receive from a deceased spouse if they were to wed again. So while college students may have been the first ones to thumb their noses at societal mores by moving in with a lover, today even some grandparents decide it's the way to go.

Close to Home

As a couple who long ago decided not to marry, this issue is a personal one for us. As children, neither of us dreamed of getting married when we grew up, possibly the legacy of our "you can do anything" feminist mothers. Our relationship was strong and felt stable and complete. We also didn't feel comfortable taking advantage of a privilege that wasn't available to many of our friends in same-sex relationships. Not getting married was an easy decision. Or so we thought.

Why Couples Live Together Without Being Married

Research shows that most couples who live together would like to get married someday, and within five years, slightly more than half of them do. Couples move in together because (obviously, not all reasons apply to all couples):

• They're in love, and they want to spend more time together.

• They want to make sure they're compatible before they make a lifetime commitment to each other. Many people we talk to say they couldn't imagine marrying someone if they hadn't lived together first.

• They're engaged to be married, and decide to move in together before the wedding.

• They're saving money for a wedding, and figure they'll live together in the meantime.

• They're spending most nights together anyway and don't want to pay two rents.

• They don't want to get married, or can't marry.

• They know their partner isn't a good match for a long-term relationship, but want to stick with this person for now.

• They would lose significant financial benefits if they were to marry. This predicament is especially common among senior citizens (who would sometimes lose a pension from a deceased spouse if they married) and disabled people.

Alternatives to Marriage Project, "Frequently Asked Questions About Cohabitation," 1998–2004, www.unmarried.org.

After we'd been living together for a few years, an occasional family member would ask if we were considering marriage. One of our employers refused to give us the type of family health insurance policy for which married couples are eligible.

Then, in 1997 there was a news story about a Rhode Island man who wanted to legally adopt the biological son of his female domestic partner, a child he'd been parenting for years and considered his son. But a Family Court judge told the man that until he married the boy's mother, he would not consider the case.

Although the story was followed closely in the Rhode Island media, there was no public outrage—no letters to the editor or courthouse protests—as there had been in similar cases affecting transracial, gay, and single-parent adoptions. It was becoming clear to us that, in spite of our large and growing numbers, unmarried people didn't see themselves as a constituency, a group that could speak out and demand equal rights.

In case we weren't convinced yet, a few months later a potential landlord suggested he would not rent to us as an unmarried couple (breaking Massachusetts state law). A month later, a tenants' insurance company informed us we would have to buy separate policies, paying double what a married couple would. Finally, we got angry enough to do what we'd been talking about for years.

We decided to found a national organization to provide resources, advocacy and support for people who choose not to marry, are unable to marry, or are in the process of deciding whether marriage is right for them. The Alternatives to Marriage Project was born, and with it the beginning of a national community where none had existed before.

Many Challenges

The conversations about what it's like to live without a ring, the challenges and the joys, are just beginning. Unmarried couples may not be harassed by hotel clerks now, but many say they still experience pressure to marry. Breckon remembers the day a newly-married friend of hers told her, "You've got to do this! Why are you holding out this back door in your relationship?"

But without marriage, Breckon says, there is a constant need to confirm her commitment to Smith. She told her friend,

"There isn't a back door. The back door isn't open. Just because we're not married doesn't mean there's an escape path."

Things often get stickiest when unmarried couples decide to have children. Relatives turn up the heat, and for many, there is internal pressure to formalize the relationship. Marie Davis, who lives in Vermont and has participated in our Alternatives to Marriage Project, hasn't decided yet whether she wants to marry her partner of three years. But she says it's hard to know whether she could resist the pressure to marry if they decided to have children.

"A friend of mine recently got pregnant," Davis says. "She was married within three or four days of telling her parents. They flew out and did this clandestine little marriage ceremony, and now they're having a big wedding. And it kind of blew me away, like whoooah, those forces are strong!"

But even this last bastion of societal expectation is slowly shifting. Studies find that about one in 10 cohabitors give birth to a child while they live together, and an additional quarter bring children from a previous relationship to the current cohabiting relationship. The newest generation of children of unmarried parents, like Arthur Prokosch, a Brown University student, say it doesn't much matter.

"It never seemed to me to be that big of a deal that my parents weren't married," he says. "I was just a kid. My parents were there. And so I never really thought about it that much."

At a time when it is common for an elementary-school classroom to include children with single, divorced, foster or adoptive, and gay and lesbian parents, children raised with two unmarried parents usually don't see fitting in as a problem. Most say the issue would come up only occasionally, in insignificant ways.

Searching his mind for a way in which his parents' lack of a marriage license affected his life, Prokosch remembers, "Every so often, [a friend] would come over and say, 'Can I have another glass of milk, Mrs. Prokosch?'" And his mother would then have to decide whether to explain that she had a different last name than Arthur and his dad and that they weren't married.

Hillary Gross, a 19-year-old from New Jersey, says she and her college friends sometimes joke about families today.

"We would tease somebody 'cause their parents are still married—'Oh, their parents are married! To each other? How weird!'"

Not Just for Heterosexuals

When one thinks of gays and lesbians and marriage, images of the recent and ongoing high-profile cases to win the right to marry often come to mind. But while many same-sex couples eagerly await their chance to . . . marry, others see themselves on the forefront of a movement pushing for a new definition of what constitutes a family.

"In my conception, what the gay and lesbian movement has been about has been tolerance of diversity," says Duncan A. Smith of Providence. Although he thinks same-sex couples should be allowed to marry, he says, "It just doesn't seem like marriage really works effectively for the majority of those who decide to marry."

Paula Ettelbrick, a New York attorney, law professor, and activist in the field of "family recognition," points out that since gay and lesbian couples haven't historically had the option of marrying, they have been forced to re-think the very notion of what a family is. "Through our success in creating different kinds of families, we have shown that groups of people can constitute a family without being heterosexual, biologically related, married, or functioning under a male head-of-household," she says. Ettelbrick says LGBT people would be better off continuing to expand how family is defined "rather than confining ourselves to marriage."

For some in the LGBT community, marriage is even more complicated. Julie Waters of Providence, a pre-operative male-to-female transsexual, is in a relationship with a woman. And right now, she can't afford the expensive surgery involved in the medical transition process.

Since she is still considered a man legally, she points out, "If I could get married to someone whose health insurance happened to cover conditions related to transsexualism, I could get the insurance through them, go through the [sex change] process, and then, in most places, the marriage would be considered null and void after the process." Situations like this demonstrate how the notion of debating whether marriage should be limited to "one man and one woman" may be missing the point.

In many ways, American society is warming to the idea that families come in many shapes and sizes. A concrete example of this is the trend toward domestic-partner benefits, an option many employers have implemented to update human-resource definitions of "family" for employees of all sexual orientations.

The most common type of discrimination unmarried people face relates to equal pay for equal work. While most employers offer health insurance to the spouse and children of an employee, it's less common for policies to be available to unmarried partners. Still, the number of companies, colleges, nonprofit organizations, and municipalities offering domestic-partner benefits to their employees is on the rise.

According to a recent poll, 6 percent of large employers now offer domestic-partner benefits, and another 29 percent say they are considering offering them. Although details vary, the plans usually require that couples have lived together for a certain amount of time and that they are jointly responsible for living expenses and are in a caring, committed relationship.

In Rhode Island, two of the top 20 largest employers offer domestic-partner benefits: Brown University and Bank-Boston. Brown implemented the benefits first, in 1994, and in addition to getting a positive response from staff, the benefits have improved the university's ability to recruit and retain employees, says Brown spokesman Mark Nickel.

As of today, Brown's definition of domestic partners is limited to same-sex partners, because the policy was developed in response to staff requests, says Nickel. "Same-sex domestic partners have almost no avenue open to them, since same-sex marriage is not legal in Rhode Island," he explains. "At least opposite-sex domestic partners have some options open to them."

But as a result of this same-sex-only policy, Breckon and Smith, a Brown employee, had to weigh their options. At one point, Breckon was in danger of being without health insurance, and Smith says they were frustrated by the fact that, if Breckon had been a same-sex partner, she could have been added to his benefits plan.

Instead, Breckon says, "Briefly, on one Thursday, we considered getting married in a hurry." Breckon, however, was able to get a job quickly, so they ultimately avoided this newest kind of shotgun wedding.

Other employers are moving in the direction of offering domestic-partner benefits that are more inclusive, defining partners without regard for gender or sexual orientation. BankBoston's plan, which took effect [in the summer of 1999], is an example. Employees now have the option of adding a spouse, dependent children, a domestic partner of any sex, or another adult dependent who meets certain criteria. "We wanted to expand eligibility with the goal to include as much of the diverse workforce as we could," says Martha Muldoon, a senior worklife consultant at BankBoston.

Los Angeles attorney Thomas Coleman is an advocate of broad-based benefits plans like BankBoston's. "I don't see why it is a legitimate business concern to an employer as to whether an opposite-sex couple chooses to be registered domestic partners rather than become legally married," he says. "If the opposite-sex couple is willing to sign the same affidavit and assume the same obligations as the employer has same-sex couples sign, then why should they not be able to do so and get the same employment benefits?"

Freedom to Choose

Despite the "family values" rallying cry of politicos, the trend away from marriage and toward less traditional families is unlikely to change anytime soon. Coleman says, "Theoretically, the Constitution protects freedom of choice in certain highly personal decisions, such as those involving marriage, family, procreation, and child-rearing." And he hopes people's freedom to choose how they will structure their families will be increasingly respected by lawmakers, courts, and businesses.

Sometimes the freedom to choose results in some unusual benefits. Prokosch, son of unmarried parents, says that when telemarketers called and asked for "Mrs. Prokosch," he could tell them honestly, "There's no one here by that name.

"That was quite convenient," he laughs.

> "*Living with someone at any point in your life may make you more prone to divorce, regardless of whether that person becomes your spouse or not.*"

Cohabitation Increases the Risk of Divorce

Stephanie Staal

Cohabitation tends to make people prone to relationship instability and divorce, argues Stephanie Staal in the following viewpoint. Couples who choose to live together may begin their cohabiting relationships too quickly and with a weaker sense of commitment than married couples do, she points out. The feelings of uncertainty that pervade such relationships often continue even if the couple decides to marry. This uncertainty, along with a decreased motivation to work through problems, can lead to marital failure, the author asserts. Staal is a newspaper reporter and the author of *The Love They Lost: Living with the Legacy of Our Parents' Divorce*.

As you read, consider the following questions:
1. What is the "cohabitation effect," according to Staal?
2. According to the author, what are the characteristics of people who choose to live together?
3. Under what circumstances does cohabitation *not* have a detrimental effect on marriage, according to Staal?

Stephanie Staal, "Warning: Living Together May Ruin Your Relationship," *Cosmopolitan*, vol. 231, September 2001, p. 286. Copyright © 2001 by The Hearst Corporation. Reproduced by permission of the author.

When Kristina Mahaffey moved in with her boyfriend of a couple months, she didn't think twice about it. After all, she was only 22, she was having fun, and it seemed like the thing to do. But her carefree attitude began to change as the reality of living together sunk in. Besides sharing a home, she and her boyfriend opened a joint bank account to pay the bills. After a few years, her family started asking her about their plans for the future. "I remember going to bed with this cloud over my head," she says. "I would think, What are we doing?" When her boyfriend proposed a few years later, Kristina was excited and said yes. "We both felt like marriage was the next step, and because we had lived together for so long, we thought we were prepared to take that step," she says. "In retrospect, if it weren't for the fact that we were living together, I probably would have said no."

The transition from live-in girlfriend to wife was not easy. Kristina had dismissed many of the problems in the relationship while they were living together—they had very different upbringings and would often reach communication impasses. Once married, those problems became harder to ignore. At the same time, her new husband started to demand that she change. "When we met, I was wild and crazy and into the dance-club scene, but all those things that were attractive to him then were suddenly a no-no once we were married," she says. "I was expected to be a different person. A year and a half into their marriage, both Kristina and her husband were so miserable that they agreed to divorce. Today, at age 34, Kristina believes that her failed marriage was due to the unanticipated pressure to marry and the false sense of compatibility resulting from their decision to cohabitate.

The Cohabitation Effect

Living together has never been as popular as it is today. The number of unmarried couples who share the same roof jumped by 72 percent in the past decade, according to the 2000 census figures. Some women, like Kristina, move in with their boyfriends for the fun and convenience of it without even considering whether they'll one day want to tie the knot. Others see shacking up as a good trial run for matrimony. According to a recent Gallup poll, 62 percent of respondents aged 20 to 29 say that living together before marriage is a good way to avoid divorce.

But the generally accepted wisdom—that living together helps determine whether the relationship is meant to be—may be erroneous. In fact, numerous studies have shown the opposite to be true. "The rate of divorce is higher—about 50 percent higher—among those who live together before marriage," says Larry Bumpass, Ph.D., professor of sociology at the University of Wisconsin. Other studies show that, for myriad reasons, living with someone at any point in your life may make you more prone to divorce, regardless of whether that person becomes your spouse or not.

Dubbed the cohabitation effect, this link between living together and relationship instability has garnered increased attention in academic circles in recent years. While the stigma attached to living together has all but faded, some experts warn that sharing a bed and a lease with a boyfriend creates far more risks than benefits to a relationship. "Based on the scientific evidence, I'd recommend people not live together," says Catherine Cohan, assistant professor of human development and family studies at Penn State University. "There is nothing to indicate that it'll help your marriage, and there is actually accumulating evidence that it could have negative consequences."

Different Theories

There are many different theories behind the cohabitation effect, but one possible explanation is that people who choose to live together have certain characteristics that make them more prone to divorce in the first place. They tend to have more liberal attitudes, are more nervous about tying the knot, and are less religious than those who don't cohabitate. "They don't see marriage as something that necessarily lasts forever, and they bring these attitudes with them into their marriages," says Paul Amato, Ph.D., a professor of sociology at Penn State University. "When things start going wrong, they might get divorced—not because their marriages are any worse but because they have fewer mental barriers to divorce."

Research also indicates that living together may actually

change people's attitudes toward marriage over time. A study that tracked people from age 18 to 23 found that the longer couples lived together, the less enthusiastic they were about family life and the fewer children they wanted to have. And the couples who lived together and then broke up were more likely to believe that it's better to get out of an unhappy marriage than to try to stick together. "Cohabitations that dissolve have a big impact on making people more positive toward divorce, because the breakups are like minidivorces," says William G. Axinn, Ph.D., a University of Michigan sociologist and lead author of the study.

The Pitfalls of Cohabitation

Particularly problematic is serial cohabitation. One study determined that the effect of cohabitation on later marital instability is found only when one or both partners had previously cohabited with someone other than their spouse. A reason for this could be that the experience of dissolving one cohabiting relationship generates a greater willingness to dissolve later relationships. People's tolerance for unhappiness is diminished, and they will scrap a marriage that might otherwise be salvaged. This may be similar to the attitudinal effects of divorce; going through a divorce makes one more tolerant of divorce.

If [these] conclusions . . . hold up under further investigation, they may hold the answer to the question of why premarital cohabitation should affect the stability of a later marriage. The act of cohabitation generates changes in people's attitudes toward marriage that make the stability of marriage less likely. Society-wide, therefore, the growth of cohabitation will tend to further weaken marriage as an institution.

David Popenoe and Barbara Dafoe Whitehead, "Should We Live Together? What Young Adults Need to Know About Cohabitation Before Marriage," National Marriage Project's Next Generation Series, 1999, www.smart marriages.com.

Abigail,[1] 30, agrees that having lived with a boyfriend for two years in her mid-20s has left a lasting negative outlook. "We had been going out for a year and a half when we decided to get our own place to see how well we worked together," she says. "Well, it became clear that we brought out

1. Some names have been changed.

the worst in each other, but I stayed in it much longer than I should have because of our living situation. And when we finally broke up, I felt so burned that I avoided any serious relationships for two years afterward. I still feel somewhat doubtful that I'll ever find The One."

The Pitfalls of a Pretend Marriage

The most compelling explanation for the cohabitation effect is that the experience of living together seems to be an incubator for potential relationship killers. Since cohabitation is not a social institution like marriage, live-in couples often do not receive the same kind of support for their relationship from their families and friends. They also usually don't get the same kind of support from each other. "An uncertain outcome of the future of the relationship might make people feel less committed," says Cohan. And as a result of that lack of commitment, couples may develop bad relationship habits during the time they live together that then persist into their marriages.

[In 1999], Cohan interviewed 92 recently married couples about their personal and marital problems and found that those who had lived together before they were married were not as good at listening to each other and solving problems together as those who hadn't. They were also more verbally aggressive toward each other. "If you're less committed to a relationship, you might be less motivated to work on your communication skills, and that decreased motivation might carry into your marriage," Cohan explains. "It might be a by-product of living together, since people in this kind of relationship often wonder Are we going to break up or are we going to get married?"

The Runaway Relationship

Indeed, yet another factor may be that living together rushes people into marriages that either happen too soon or shouldn't be happening at all. "Cohabitation is seen as more casual—people are moving in with someone with much less consideration than they would if they were marrying that person," says Linda Waite, University of Chicago sociologist and coauthor of *The Case for Marriage*. "They don't realize that these situations are hard to get out of emotionally and financially, and so these poorly considered choices often become marriages. If people went more slowly, it would be easier to back up and break things off."

Sarah, 26, found that her relationship with her boyfriend Rick took on a momentum of its own as soon as they moved in together. "We felt a lot of pressure to figure out where things were going," she says. A few months later, they became engaged. With the stress of planning a wedding, Sarah had little time to focus on her uneasiness about getting married to Rick. "I even had misgivings when I was walking down the aisle," she says. Her doubts turned out to be well-founded. Two years later, she and Rick separated. Looking back, Sarah can see how living together pushed her into marrying someone who was not a good match. "If we had just been dating, I would've been able to see him more clearly and not as someone I need something from or have to negotiate with because we're living together," says Sarah.

When Living Together Lasts

While social scientists continue to research the cohabitation effect, many are quick to point out that not all unmarried couples are alike. Certain factors, such as the level of commitment and religious beliefs, can help predict the long-range success of the relationship. "It's the way couples go into their relationships that affects the level of stability you see in their marriages," says health scientist and demographer Lynne Casper. "I think treating cohabitants as one single entity can be problematic."

One group that seems to be exempt from the cohabitation effect are couples who are engaged or have definite plans to marry before they move in together. A 1996 study found that relationship quality did not differ between these couples and successfully married couples. "The people whom we have to be concerned about are the serial cohabitants," says Susan Brown, Ph.D., a sociologist at Bowling Green State University and lead author of the study. "Those are the kind of people who are going to have poorer relationship skills and an inability to sustain intimate relationships."

So should you or shouldn't you? If you're considering it,

know that one major success factor is to discuss openly and agree upon what your hopes for living together are to prevent any misunderstandings or resentment down the road. "It is really important for both parties to be clear about what they expect," says Dorian Solot, executive director of the Alternatives to Marriage Project, an advocacy group for unmarried couples. "A surprising number of people move in together where one partner expects to get married soon and the other one doesn't. That sets the stage for all sorts of trouble."

When Sophie, 28, first suggested to her boyfriend Scott that they live together, she was stunned when he said no. "We had been dating seriously for two years, and I was really upset, but then we talked about what living together meant. He explained that he saw it as a step toward marriage and he wasn't sure he was ready," she says. "It was interesting, because I didn't see it that way." So for the next six months, they continued to talk it over until they finally decided to live together with the intention of getting married when the time was right. "I wanted to move in together because I wanted more of a commitment. But I now see that if we had jumped in it too soon, it could have driven us apart."

| *"Only marriage can bring [a gay person] home."*

Marriage Should Be Available to Gays and Lesbians

Andrew Sullivan

In the following viewpoint Andrew Sullivan shares a personal story to illustrate the importance of gay marriage. Sullivan experienced withdrawal and depression as he became aware of his homosexuality during his teen years. Because it seemed that married life would never be available to him, he rejected the idea of family and marriage and had difficulty forming a committed relationship with another man. When gays and lesbians are denied the right to civil marriage, it devalues their love and cuts them off from a stable family life, states Sullivan. Sullivan is a senior editor at the *New Republic*.

As you read, consider the following questions:
1. What kind of home did Sullivan grow up in?
2. What did the author do to avoid confronting the reality about his sexual orientation during his high school years?
3. In Sullivan's opinion, what rights do churches have concerning marriage between gays and lesbians?

Andrew Sullivan, "Why the *M* Word Matters to Me," *Time*, vol. 163, February 16, 2004, p. 104. Copyright © 2004 by Time, Inc. All rights reserved. Reproduced by permission.

As a child, I had no idea what homosexuality was. I grew up in a traditional home—Catholic, conservative, middle class. Life was relatively simple: education, work, family. I was raised to aim high in life, even though my parents hadn't gone to college. But one thing was instilled in me. What mattered was not how far you went in life, how much money you earned, how big a name you made for yourself. What really mattered was family and the love you had for one another. The most important day of your life was not graduation from college or your first day at work or a raise or even your first house. The most important day of your life was when you got married. It was on that day that all your friends and all your family got together to celebrate the most important thing in life: your happiness—your ability to make a new home, to form a new but connected family, to find love that put everything else into perspective.

But as I grew older, I found that this was somehow not available to me. I didn't feel the things for girls that my peers did. All the emotions and social rituals and bonding of teenage heterosexual life eluded me. I didn't know why. No one explained it. My emotional bonds to other boys were one-sided; each time I felt myself falling in love, they sensed it, pushed it away. I didn't and couldn't blame them. I got along fine with my buds in a nonemotional context, but something was awry, something not right. I came to know almost instinctively that I would never be a part of my family the way my siblings might one day be. The love I had inside me was unmentionable, anathema. I remember writing in my teenage journal one day, "I'm a professional human being. But what do I do in my private life?"

I never discussed my real life. I couldn't date girls and so immersed myself in schoolwork, the debate team, school plays, anything to give me an excuse not to confront reality. When I looked toward the years ahead, I couldn't see a future. There was just a void. Was I going to be alone my whole life? Would I ever have a most important day in my life? It seemed impossible, a negation, an undoing. To be a full part of my family, I had to somehow not be me. So, like many other gay teens, I withdrew, became neurotic, depressed, at times close to suicidal. I shut myself in my room with my books night after night while my peers developed the skills needed to form real relationships and loves. In wounded pride, I even voiced a rejection of family and marriage. It was the only way I could explain my isolation.

Sargent. © 2004 by Universal Press Syndicate. Reproduced by permission.

It took years for me to realize that I was gay, years more to tell others and more time yet to form any kind of stable emotional bond with another man. Because my sexuality had emerged in solitude—and without any link to the idea of an actual relationship—it was hard later to reconnect sex to love and self-esteem. It still is. But I persevered, each relationship slowly growing longer than the last, learning in my 20s and 30s what my straight friends had found out in their teens. But even then my parents and friends never asked the question they would have asked automatically if I were straight: So, when are you going to get married? When will we be able to celebrate it and affirm it and support it? In fact, no one—no one—has yet asked me that question.

When people talk about gay marriage, they miss the point. This isn't about gay marriage. It's about marriage. It's about family. It's about love. It isn't about religion. It's about *civil* marriage licenses. Churches can and should have the right to say no to marriage for gays in their congregations, just as Catholics say no to divorce, but divorce is still a civil option. These family values are not options for a happy and stable life. They are necessities. Putting gay relationships in some other category—civil unions, domestic partnerships, whatever—may alleviate real human needs, but by their very euphemism, by their very separateness, they actually build a wall between gay people and their families. They put back the barrier many of us have spent a lifetime trying to erase.

It's too late for me to undo my past. But I want above everything else to remember a young kid out there who may even be reading this now. I want to let him know that he doesn't have to choose between himself and his family anymore. I want him to know that his love has dignity, that he does indeed have a future as a full and equal part of the human race. Only marriage will do that. Only marriage can bring him home.

"Marriage as the union of male and female has been part of the common currency of humanity for millennia."

Marriage Should Unite One Man and One Woman

Alliance for Marriage

Americans must reaffirm marriage as an institution that unites one man and one woman to create a stable family, contends the Alliance for Marriage in the following viewpoint. In recent years analysts have noted that family disintegration is likely the root cause of serious social problems such as crime and poverty. The family is being undermined by activist groups who are attempting to change the time-tested definition of marriage as the union of two genders, the authors argue. Since traditional marriage is essential for the health of children and society, concerned citizens should support a federal amendment to protect marriage. The Alliance for Marriage is an organization dedicated to defending the traditional concept of marriage and family.

As you read, consider the following questions:
1. What is the public consensus regarding the nature of marriage, in the authors' opinion?
2. According to the Alliance for Marriage, what have activist groups done in an attempt to redefine marriage?
3. What is the text of the proposed Federal Marriage Amendment, according to the authors?

In July of [2001], we gathered in Washington to call upon leaders of Congress to defend both marriage and democracy in America by introducing a constitutional amendment designed to preserve the legal status of marriage for future generations. Specifically, we called upon Congress to introduce the Federal Marriage Amendment that has been drafted by the Alliance for Marriage.

As a coalition representing the vast majority of Americans who believe in marriage, we maintain that the future of marriage and the family in America is greater than any issue of partisan politics. And so we are very pleased that a bi-partisan group of leaders in Congress has responded to our call to defend the right of the American people to determine for themselves—and for their children and grandchildren—the nature and definition of marriage under American law.

The Alliance for Marriage

The Alliance for Marriage is a non-partisan research and education organization dedicated to promoting marriage and addressing the crisis of family disintegration in the United States. We are a racially and culturally diverse coalition whose membership reflects the fact that marriage is the most multicultural social institution in the world.

We represent several of the largest African-American denominations in the United States. We represent millions of Latinos and Asian Americans. We represent Jews, Christians and Muslims from every ethnic background. And finally, we represent the vast majority of Americans who share a deep consensus—consistently reflected in polls and statewide referenda—regarding the unique nature and social importance of marriage as the union of male and female.

We are Americans of every color and every creed who share a commitment to reducing the epidemic of family breakdown and restoring a marriage-based culture in the United States. Some of us are Democrats. Some of us are Republicans. And many of us do not belong to any political party. But we all share the fundamental conviction that the tragedy of family disintegration in America is a greater national priority than any matter of partisan politics.

For several decades, America has been wandering in a

wilderness of social problems caused by family disintegration. And an overwhelming body of social science data has established that America's greatest social problems—violent crime, welfare dependency, and child poverty—track more closely with family disintegration than they do with any other social variable, including race and income level.

Affirming the Natural Family

• *We affirm* that the natural family, not the individual, is the fundamental unit of society.

• *We affirm* that natural family to be the union of a man and a woman for the purposes of sharing love and joy, propagating children, providing their moral education, building a vital home economy, offering security in times of trouble, and binding the generations.

• *We affirm* that the natural family is a fixed aspect of the created order, one ingrained in human nature. Distinct family systems may grow weaker or stronger. However, the natural family cannot change into some new shape; nor can it be re-defined by eager social engineers. . . .

• *We affirm* the marital union to be the authentic sexual bond, the only one open to the natural and responsible creation of new life.

Allan C. Carlson and Paul T. Mero, "The Natural Family: A Manifesto," *Family in America*, March 2005.

Tragically, as bad as our current situation may be, it could soon become dramatically worse. This is because the courts in America are poised to erase the legal road map to marriage and the family from American law. In fact, the weakening of the legal status of marriage in America at the hands of the courts has already begun. This process represents nothing less than a profoundly anti-democratic social revolution—advancing apart from the democratic process and against the will of a clear majority of the American people. If allowed to continue, this revolution will deprive future generations of Americans of the legal road map that they will need to have a fighting chance of finding their way out of the social wilderness of family disintegration.

Marriage as the union of male and female has been part of

the common currency of humanity for millennia. In fact, marriage as the union of the two genders is literally the most multicultural social institution in the world—cutting across all racial, cultural and religious lines. This is because marriage as the union of male and female has unique and irreplaceable benefits for both children and society.

The institution of marriage is so central to the well being of both children and our society that it was, until recently, difficult to imagine that marriage itself would need explicit constitutional protection. However, our country's time-honored understanding that the very essence of marriage is the union of male and female has come under fire in the courts.

For years, the American people, acting through the democratic process at the state level, have been forced to repeatedly defend the deep public consensus regarding the nature and definition of marriage from being undermined by activist organizations attempting a social revolution through the courts. Activist groups openly acknowledge that their goal is to use the courts to force the redefinition of marriage upon the American people within five to ten years. And recent developments amply confirm that the process of using the courts to undermine the legal status of marriage in America is already well advanced.

The Need for a Constitutional Amendment

It has become increasingly clear that neither our state laws defining marriage, nor the federal Defense of Marriage Act,[1] will withstand the multiple challenges to the legal status of marriage that have been, and will continue to be, unleashed in both the state and federal courts. A critical juncture has been reached. And the time has come for Congress to put this issue back where it belongs—in the hands of the American people.

Indeed, developments in the courts have brought our nation to a historic crossroads. The progressive weakening of marriage is now so far advanced that we can no longer hope to preserve the legal status of marriage for future genera-

1. This 1996 act gives states the right to refuse to recognize same-sex marriages licensed in other states.

tions short of using the ultimate democratic tool available to the American people—a federal constitutional amendment.

The Federal Marriage Amendment

The text of the Federal Marriage Amendment reads:

> Marriage in the United States shall consist only of the union of a man and a woman. Neither this constitution or the constitution of any state, nor state or federal law, shall be construed to require that marital status or the legal incidents thereof be conferred upon unmarried couples or groups.

The first sentence simply states that marriage in the United States consists of the union of male and female. The second sentence ensures that the democratic process at the state level will continue to determine the allocation of the benefits traditionally associated with marriage. State legislatures retain authority to legislate in the area of marital benefits. But the courts are precluded from distorting existing constitutional or statutory law into a requirement that marital status or the legal incidents thereof be reallocated pursuant to a judicial decree.

The Federal Marriage Amendment is thus narrowly tailored to address negative developments in the courts. The amendment is a reasonable embodiment of the deep public consensus regarding the unique nature and social importance of marriage as the union of male and female. At the same time, the amendment returns to the democratic process at the state level authority that is currently being usurped by the courts at the request of activist organizations.

In short, the Federal Marriage Amendment is a reasonable response to the crisis for our democratic society created by those who would use the courts to overcome public opinion with respect to marriage. Gays and lesbians have a right to live as they choose. But they don't have a right to redefine marriage for our entire society.

It is very important to remember that activist organizations and the courts are the ones responsible for constitutionalizing the issue of the legal status of marriage. The entire effort to undermine the legal status of marriage in the courts is premised upon constitutional law. For example, activist organizations openly admit their plans to use the Equal Protection and Full Faith and Credit clauses of the United States Constitution to eventually impose same-sex "marriage" and "civil unions" on every state in the nation. The only question is whether the constitutional status of marriage will be determined by unelected judges or the American people.

Protecting Marriage for Future Generations

No one involved in the Alliance for Marriage believes that saving the legal status of marriage in America will *alone* be sufficient to stem the tide of family disintegration in our country. But we are convinced that protecting the legal status of marriage—and in the process protecting the right of the American people to decide critical issues of social policy for themselves—is a *necessary* condition for the renewal of a marriage-based culture in the United States.

This is a great nation. We can do better than accept astronomical rates of youth crime and child poverty because of an epidemic of family disintegration. But our nation cannot go forward unless our laws send a positive message to our children about marriage, family and their future. This is why the Alliance for Marriage has created the Federal Marriage Amendment—to allow Americans to pass the legal roadmap for marriage and the family on to future generations.

Periodical Bibliography

The following articles have been selected to supplement the diverse views presented in this chapter.

Balfour Brickner	"The Death of the Nuclear Family: Towards a New Sexual Ethic in America," *Conscience*, Summer 2004.
Susan Dominus	"Growing Up with Mom and Mom," *New York Times Magazine*, October 24, 2004.
Forecast	"What Happened to the Wedding Bells?" April 2003.
Jennifer Gaboury	"Saying 'I Don't,'" *SIECUS Report*, Winter 2005.
Maggie Gallagher	"Latter Day Federalists: Why We Need a National Definition of Marriage," *Weekly Standard*, March 29, 2004.
Judith Hayes	"The Purity Ring: How a Simple Gift Can Change Your Child's Life," *Christian Parenting Today*, January/February 2002.
John S. James	"Virginity Pledge Did Not Prevent Sexually Transmitted Infections," *AIDS Treatment News*, February 25, 2005.
Kenneth Jost	"Gay Marriage," *CQ Researcher*, September 5, 2003.
William J. O'Malley	"Understanding Sex Before Sin," *America*, September 23, 2002.
Leland D. Peterson	"May You Live to See Your Children's Children," *New Oxford Review*, November 2004.
Katha Pollitt	"Adam and Steve—Together at Last," *Nation*, December 15, 2003.
Emily Sellers Roberts	"No Regrets: It Wasn't Easy Staying Abstinent for 23 Years, but Here's Why I'm Glad I Did," *Today's Christian Woman*, September/October 2002.
Rosemary Radford Ruether	"Sexual Illiteracy," *Conscience*, Summer 2003.
Lauren Weedon	"These Women May Look Sexy . . . but They Don't Have Sex," *Marie Claire*, June 2003.
Phyllis H. Witcher	"Not-So-Cozy Cohabitation," *World & I*, March 2004.
David Von Drehle and Alan Cooperman	"A Fast-Moving Movement," *Washington Post Weekly Edition*, March 15–21, 2004.

CHAPTER 3

How Should Sex Education Be Conducted?

Chapter Preface

Starting in the mid-1990s, the U.S. Congress authorized federal funding for state-run programs that encourage unmarried minors to refrain from sexual activity. Participating states have applied the funding in various ways, from supporting local youth organizations that promote abstinence to creating media campaigns that encourage parents to discuss sex with their children. Most states have split the federal money among several approaches. Since 1997, however, many political leaders have promoted school-based sex education that teaches that the societal norm for sexual activity is "mutually faithful monogamous heterosexual relationships in the context of marriage." Federally funded school programs must, in fact, promote abstinence exclusively and avoid advocating contraceptives and "safer sex" strategies for preventing sexually transmitted diseases. Parents, educators, and students have had mixed reactions to the implementation of abstinence-only education in schools.

Promoters of the federally approved programs contend that the consequences of teen pregnancy and the proliferation of sexually transmitted diseases (STDs) among youth warrant an abstinence-only message. Joe S. McIlaney, president of the Medical Institute for Sexual Health, contends that schools have a duty to promote abstinence as the one certain way for teens to avoid pregnancy and disease. In his opinion, teaching students so-called "safer sex" techniques, such as the use of condoms, is irresponsible because condoms are not risk-free. He asserts that condoms have been shown to be only partially effective against herpes and chlamydia and ineffective against the human papilloma virus (HPV) that causes genital warts. "Students must not leave the . . . classroom thinking, 'I'm being responsible and safe if I use a condom,'" insists McIlaney. "The school's message must be absolutely clear: 'There is no responsible sex for unmarried teenagers.'"

Many public health officials, however, believe that comprehensive sex education that includes accurate information about contraceptives and STD prevention is the best way to protect youths from the risks of sex. Cory Richards, senior vice president at the Alan Guttmacher Institute, argues that public schools should certainly teach youths about the benefits of delaying sexual activity and resisting peer pressure to have sex. But he maintains that abstinence-only programs that denigrate the effectiveness of condoms and contraceptives are misleading and even dangerous. Richards argues, "Undermining people's confidence in the effectiveness of condoms and other contraceptive methods as a means of scaring them out of having sex is just plain wrong. Protecting our young people requires a balanced approach that emphasizes all the key means of prevention including effective contraception and condom use, as well as delaying sex."

Many recent surveys suggest that most Americans would prefer sex-education programs that offer a kind of "middle way" between abstinence-only approaches and contraception-driven curricula. According to the National Campaign to Prevent Teen Pregnancy, "The overwhelming majority of Americans . . . support a strong emphasis on abstinence as the best option for teens by far, coupled with information about contraception. They continue to reject the notion that it's *either* abstinence or contraception. Unfortunately, these middle-ground views are often drowned out by the polarizing arguments surrounding the contentious issue of teen pregnancy."

These differences of opinion among policy makers, health officials, and the public are likely to remain sources of heated debate in the years to come as politicians revisit the issue of federally funded sex education. The authors of the following viewpoints offer a variety of perspectives on what sexual values schools should emphasize.

"Only when abstinence education began in recent years did the numbers of sexually active teens go down."

Abstinence-Only Programs Benefit Youths

Kathleen Tsubata

Kathleen Tsubata, codirector of the Washington AIDS International Foundation, teaches HIV/AIDS prevention in public schools and community venues. In the following viewpoint Tsubata contends that programs that teach students to abstain from sexual activity until marriage have helped to lower teen pregnancy rates. More importantly, she argues, only abstinence from sex can protect youths from life-threatening diseases such as AIDS. This kind of education should be fully supported and federally funded, she concludes.

As you read, consider the following questions:

1. What is problematic about teaching youths to use condoms to prevent HIV infections, in Tsubata's opinion?
2. According to a February 2003 Zogby poll cited by the author, what percentage of parents prefer abstinence education?
3. According to Tsubata, what are the various non-health-related benefits of teaching youths to abstain from sex?

Kathleen Tsubata, "Yes: Abstinence Is Working to Decrease Teen Pregnancy and Is Building Character Among Our Nation's Youth," *Insight on the News*, November 10, 2003, p. 46. Copyright © 2003 by News World Communications, Inc. All rights reserved. Reproduced by permission.

The current tug-of-war between "abstinence-only" and "comprehensive" sexual-education advocates is distracting us from the real issue. We are in a war against forces far more unforgiving than we ever have encountered. We must look at what works to save lives. My work brings me to deal with teens every day, in public schools, churches and community organizations, teaching HIV/AIDS prevention. I train teens to teach others about this genocidal plague that is sweeping nations around the world and depleting continents of their most-productive population. I can tell you that most teens have a very superficial understanding of HIV and that many are putting themselves at risk in a wide variety of ways.

While teen pregnancy is serious, it is still, in one sense, the lesser evil. It's a difficult thing to bear a child out of wedlock, with the accompanying loss of education, financial stability and freedom. However, compared to HIV, it's a walk in the park. Make no mistake about it: The choice of sexual activity is a life-and-death matter, as Third World nations are finding out in stark terms.

The Problem with Condoms

Having multiple sexual partners is the No. 1 risk factor for contracting HIV and 19 percent of teens have had four or more sexual partners.

"So teach them to use condoms!" we are told. Studies indicate that condoms, if used correctly and consistently, may lower the transmission rate to 15 to 25 percent. That's not a fail-safe guarantee, as any condom manufacturer under litigation quickly would point out.

But there are two additional problems with condoms being the central pillar of HIV prevention. First, correct usage of condoms is hard to achieve in the dimly lit, cramped back seat of a car. Second, and more importantly, kids simply make decisions differently than adults. Janet St. Lawrence, of the Centers for Disease Control and Prevention (CDC), related the results of one behavioral study to me in a phone conversation [in 2002]. In that study, teens reported using a condom for their first sexual contact with someone, and subsequent contacts, "until they felt the relationship was permanent," St. Lawrence said. Then they stopped using condoms. These teens were asked what defines a "permanent" relationship. "Lasting 21 days or longer," was their response. In other words, such a teen could start a relationship, initiate sex using a condom, decide after three weeks that it is "safe" to stop using a condom, break up and replay the whole cycle, convinced that this was responsible sexual behavior.

Teens are not realistic because they are young and not fully developed in key mental and emotional areas. They tend to imbue love with magical properties, as if the emotion is a sanitizing force, and that their trust can be shown by the willingness to take risks. Kids process information differently than adults. Parents know this. Saying "It's best not to have sex, but if you do, use a condom" is translated in their minds to "It's okay to have sex if you use a condom." Then, if they feel "this is true love," they convince themselves that even that is unnecessary. That's why during four decades of sex education we witnessed steep increases in sexual activity and the consequential increases in teen pregnancy, sexually transmitted diseases and poverty.

The Benefits of Abstinence Education

Only when abstinence education began in recent years did the numbers of sexually active teens go down a full 8 percentage points from 54 percent of teens to 46 percent, according to the 2001 *Youth Risk Behavior Surveillance*, published by the CDC. Simultaneously, teen pregnancies went down, abortions went down and condom use went up among those who were sexually active. Raising the bar to establish abstinence as the best method indirectly resulted in more-responsible behavior in general.

You would think such good news would have people dancing in the aisles. Instead, the safe-sex gurus grimly predict that increased abstinence education will result in teens giving in to natural urges without the benefit of latex. Or, the critics of abstinence-until-marriage education insisted that their programs (which pay lip service to abstinence) somehow reached teens more effectively than the programs that focused on abstinence. A third interpretation is that contraception, not abstinence, has lowered the numbers.

However, a study of lowered teen-pregnancy rates between

1991 and 1995 (published in *Adolescent and Family Health* by Mohn, Tingle et al., April 2003) showed that abstinence, not contraceptives, was the major cause of the lowered pregnancy rate. Another 1996 study, by John Vessey, of Northwestern University Medical School, followed up on 2,541 teens, ages 13 to 16, who completed an abstinence-education program. He reported that one year after completing the program, 54 percent of formerly sexually active teens no longer were sexually active. This puts to rest the idea that "once a teen has sex, they will continue to be sexually active."

Support for Abstinence-Only Education

Those who support using abstinence-only curricula say that abstinence is the only 100% effective method of preventing unintended pregnancies and STD infections. Since abstinence is the only method that can never fail—condoms break and even birth control pills have been known to fail and do nothing to protect against disease—it is the only one that should be presented to students, they say.

Teaching students the notion of "safer sex," supporters say, is a fallacy and only gives students a false sense of security. "Studies have shown that condoms are not always effective at preventing pregnancy and sexually transmitted diseases including HIV," according to Concerned Women for America, a conservative, religion-based women's advocacy group. "Moreover, herpes, syphilis, and the 'silent' STDs . . . can be spread to men and women through contact with the skin of an infected individual—something condoms can't guard against."

Issues & Controversies On File, "Abstinence-Only Education," May 24, 2002.

It often is claimed that most parents want pro-contraceptive education for their kids. In fact, a nationwide Zogby International poll of 1,245 parents in February [2003] (see poll results at www.whatparentsthink.com) commissioned by the pro-abstinence Coalition for Adolescent Sexual Health found that when shown the actual content of both comprehensive and abstinence-only sex-education programs, 73 percent of parents supported abstinence education and 75 percent opposed the condom-based education, with 61 percent opposing the comprehensive sex-ed programs.

But what do teens themselves think? In a 2000 study by the National Campaign to Prevent Teen Pregnancy, 93 percent of the teens surveyed said there should be a strong message from society not to engage in sex at least until graduation from high school. Will abstinence education cause sexually active teens to be unable to find out about contraception? The small amount in abstinence-education funding requested by Congress ($135 million among three programs) is miniscule compared with the $379 million funding of only six of the 25 federal programs teaching contraceptive-based education. This is Goliath complaining that David is using up all the rocks.

But, in all good conscience, can we teach something that would put kids in danger of contracting HIV, even if at a somewhat-reduced risk? Can we glibly decide, "Oh, only 15 percent of users will die?" That's acceptable? The stakes simply are too high. Even one life is too important to lose. When we're talking about life and death, we can't settle for the soggy argument of "Kids are going to do it anyway." That's what used to be said about racial discrimination, drunk driving and cigarette smoking, but when people became serious about countering these behaviors, they receded. If we realize the necessity of saving every teen's life, we can't help but teach them that because sex is wonderful, powerful and life-changing, it must be treated with great care.

The Need to Limit Sexuality

Sex is most pleasurable and joyful when there is no fear of disease, when both partners feel absolute trust in the other, when the possibility of a pregnancy is not a destructive one and when each person truly wants the best for the other. This takes self-development, investment, emotional growth, responsibility and a whole host of other elements a typical teen doesn't possess, unless they are guided. In reality, every person already is aware of the need to limit sexuality to certain times and places, like many activities. Sexuality is far more complex than the physical mechanics of orgasm. That stuff is pretty much automatic. It's far more important to know that orgasm is the perfectly engineered system for creating life, and for experiencing the fulfillment of love.

Abstinence isn't a vague ideal but a practical, feasible life skill. Studies show that kids who are able to say no to sex also can say no to drugs, alcohol and tobacco. The skills in one area automatically transfer to other areas of health. Learning to delay gratification can have positive impacts on academic goals and athletic accomplishments.

Without the soap-opera distractions of sex, kids feel more confident and free to enjoy the process of making friends, developing their own individuality and working on their dreams. That's why virtually no one looks back on the decision to be sexually abstinent and says "I wish I had never done that." But 63 percent of teen respondents who have had sex regretted it and said they wish they had waited, according to an International Communications Research of Media survey in June 2000 commissioned by the National Campaign to Prevent Teen Pregnancy. Further, 78 percent of the 12- to 17-year-old respondents said teens should not be sexually active, and only 21 percent thought sex for teens was okay if they used birth control.

Youths Want Support

Teens are telling us that they need support to resist the pressure to have sex. Even just making an abstinence pledge was found to delay sexual debut by 18 months on average, according to the National Longitudinal Study on Adolescent Health in 1997. And teens who know their parents have a strong belief and expectation of abstinence are far more likely to abstain, as shown in two 2002 studies released by the University of Minnesota Center for Adolescent Health and Development in which more than 80 percent of teens stayed abstinent when they knew their mothers strongly disapproved of premarital sex.

Even if it were only to end the spread of HIV/AIDS, that would be a valid reason to support abstinence education.

But teaching abstinence goes beyond preventing disease and unwanted pregnancy. It helps kids improve in the areas of self-esteem, academic attainments and future careers. It increases refusal skills toward drugs, alcohol and smoking. It equips teens with tools that they will use successfully throughout life, especially in their eventual marriage and family life. In other words, it has a positive ripple effect both in terms of their current and future life courses.

In my estimation, that definitely is worth funding.

*"Studies have found that abstinence-only
education does not appear to decrease teen
pregnancy or the risk of sexually
transmitted diseases."*

Abstinence-Only Programs Teach False Information

Congressional Committee on Government Reform

In 2004 California Democratic representative Henry A. Waxman requested a congressional committee to investigate the content of federally funded abstinence-only sex education programs. The following viewpoint is excerpted from the committee's report, which found that the majority of abstinence-only curricula contain false, misleading, or distorted information about reproductive health. The authors state that such programs often downplay the effectiveness of condoms in preventing sexually transmitted diseases and pregnancy. These curricula also blur religion and science and treat gender stereotypes as facts, the committee found. Students enrolled in abstinence-only programs are not likely to make informed decisions about their sexual health, the authors maintain.

As you read, consider the following questions:
1. What facts do abstinence-only programs fail to report about consistent condom use, according to the authors?
2. According to the report, in what ways do abstinence-only curricula blur religion and science?
3. What kinds of scientific errors can be found in abstinence-only programs, according to the authors?

U.S. House Committee on Government Reform—Minority Staff, Special Investigations Division, "The Content of Federally Funded Abstinence-Only Education Programs," prepared for Rep. Henry A. Waxman, December 2004.

U nder the Bush Administration, there has been a dramatic increase in federal support for "abstinence-only" education programs. Also called "abstinence education" or "abstinence-until-marriage education," these programs promote abstinence from all sexual activity, usually until marriage, as the only way to reduce the risks of pregnancy, disease, and other potential consequences of sex. The programs define sexual activity broadly and do not teach basic facts about contraception.

In fiscal year 2001, under the last budget passed under the Clinton Administration, abstinence-only education programs received approximately $80 million in federal funding. Since then, federal abstinence-only funding has more than doubled, with the final omnibus appropriations bill containing $167 million in funding for fiscal year 2005. President [George W.] Bush had proposed $270 million for abstinence-only programs in fiscal year 2005. . . .

What Researchers Have Found

There have been several studies of the effectiveness of abstinence-only education. These studies have found that abstinence-only education does not appear to decrease teen pregnancy or the risk of sexually transmitted diseases [STDs]. In the most comprehensive analysis of teen pregnancy prevention programs, researchers found that "the few rigorous studies of abstinence-only curricula that have been completed to date do not show any overall effect on sexual behavior or contraceptive use."

One recent study of abstinence-only programs found that they may actually increase participants' risk. Columbia University researchers found that while virginity "pledge" programs helped some participants to delay sex, 88% still had premarital sex, and their rates of sexually transmitted diseases showed no statistically significant difference from those of nonpledgers. Virginity pledgers were also less likely to use contraception when they did have sex and were less likely to seek STD testing despite comparable infection rates.

In contrast, comprehensive sex education that both encourages abstinence and teaches about effective contraceptive use has been shown in many studies to delay sex, reduce the frequency of sex, and increase the use of condoms and other contraceptives. . . .

False and Misleading Information

Under the SPRANS [Special Projects of Regional and National Significance] requirements, abstinence-only education programs are not allowed to teach their participants any methods to reduce the risk of pregnancy other than abstaining until marriage. They are allowed to mention contraceptives only to describe their failure rates. Although the curricula purport to provide scientifically accurate information about contraceptive failure rates, many exaggerate these failure rates, providing affirmatively false or misleading information that misstates the effectiveness of various contraceptive methods in preventing disease transmission or pregnancy.

• *HIV prevention.* According to the Centers for Disease Control and Prevention (CDC), "Latex condoms, when used consistently and correctly, are highly effective in preventing the transmission of HIV, the virus that causes AIDS." Contrary to this scientific consensus, multiple curricula provide false information about condoms and HIV transmission.

Several curricula cite an erroneous 1993 study of condom effectiveness that has been discredited by federal health officials. The 1993 study, by Dr. Susan Weller, looked at a variety of condom effectiveness studies and concluded that condoms reduce HIV transmission by 69%. Dr. Weller's conclusions were rejected by the Department of Health and Human Services, which issued a statement in 1997 informing the public that "FDA [Food and Drug Administration] and CDC believe this analysis was flawed." The Department cited numerous methodological problems, including the mixing of data on consistent condom use with data on inconsistent condom use, and found that Dr. Weller's calculation of a 69% effectiveness rate was based on "serious error." In fact, CDC noted that "[o]ther studies of discordant couples—more recent and larger than the ones Weller reviewed, and conducted over several years—have demonstrated that consistent condom use is highly effective at preventing HIV infection.". . .

• *Prevention of other STDs.* Several curricula distort public health data on the effectiveness of condoms in preventing other sexually transmitted diseases. One curriculum claims: "If condoms were effective against STDs, it would be reasonable to expect that an increase in condom usage would correlate to a decrease in STDs overall—which is not the case. Rather, as condom usage has increased, so have rates of STDs." Another states: "[T]he popular claim that 'condoms help prevent the spread of STDs,' is not supported by the data."

These assertions are wrong. The curricula fail to note that rates of important sexually transmitted diseases, such as syphilis and gonorrhea, have been dropping over the past decade. Contrary to the assertions in the curricula, the most recent data show that consistent condom use is associated with:

- Reduced acquisition of syphilis by women and by men;
- Reduced acquisition of gonorrhea by women;
- Reduced acquisition of urethral infection by men; and
- Faster regression of HPV [human papilloma virus] related lesions on the cervix and penis, and faster clearance of genital HPV infection in women.

The assertions in the curricula are presented next to a chart of "Increasing Condom Usage" alongside a chart showing increased rates of chlamydia over the same time period. Yet in the case of chlamydia, CDC attributes the increase in reported infection rates to increased detection because of "increased screening, recognition of asymptomatic infection (mainly in women), and improved reporting, as well as the continuing high burden of disease." Indeed, both CDC and independent experts have found that condoms can reduce the risk of chlamydia infection.

Condoms and Pregnancy Prevention

None of the curricula provides information on how to select a birth control method and use it effectively. However, several curricula exaggerate condom failure rates in preventing pregnancy.

Failure rates for contraception are calculated as the probability of a couple experiencing pregnancy when relying primarily on the contraceptive method over the course of one year. "Typical use" failure rates are often higher than "perfect use" rates largely because the former include people who use the method incorrectly or only sometimes. Condoms have a typical use contraceptive failure rate of approximately 15% and a perfect use failure rate of 2% to 3%.

According to the World Health Organization, the difference between typical and perfect use "is due primarily to inconsistent and incorrect use, not to condom failure. Condom failure—the device breaking or slipping off during intercourse—is uncommon."

Kirk. © 1990 by Kirk Anderson. Reproduced by permission.

Several curricula misrepresent the data to exaggerate how often condoms fail to prevent pregnancy:

- The parent guide for one curriculum understates condom effectiveness by falsely describing "actual use" as "scrupulous." It states: "When used by real people in real-life situations, research confirms that 14 percent of the women who use condoms scrupulously for birth control become pregnant within a year." In fact, for couples who use condoms "scrupulously," the 2% to 3% failure rate applies.
- Two other curricula understate condom effectiveness by neglecting to explain that failure rates represent the chance of pregnancy over the course of a year. One states: "Couples who use condoms to avoid a pregnancy

have a failure rate of 15%." The other claims: "The typical failure rate for the male condom is 14% in preventing pregnancy." These statements inaccurately suggest that the chance of pregnancy is 14% to 15% after each act of protected intercourse. In addition, they do not make clear that most condom "failure" is due to incorrect or inconsistent use.

Another curriculum presents misleading information about the risk of pregnancy from sexual activity other than intercourse. The curriculum erroneously states that touching another person's genitals "can result in pregnancy." In fact, the source cited for this contention specifically states that "remaining a virgin all but eliminates the possibility of becoming pregnant.". . .

Blurring Religion and Science

By their nature, abstinence-only curricula teach moral judgments alongside scientific facts. The SPRANS program mandates, for example, that programs teach that having sex only within marriage "is the expected standard of human sexual activity." In some of the curricula, the moral judgments are explicitly religious. For example, in a newsletter accompanying one popular curriculum, the author laments that as a result of societal change, "No longer were we valued as spiritual beings made by a loving Creator." The curriculum's author closes the section by signing, "In His Service."

In other curricula, moral judgments are misleadingly offered as scientific fact.

Although religions and moral codes offer different answers to the question of when life begins, some abstinence-only curricula present specific religious views on this question as scientific fact. One curriculum teaches: "Conception, also known as fertilization, occurs when one sperm unites with one egg in the upper third of the fallopian tube. This is when life begins." Another states: "Fertilization (or conception) occurs when one of the father's sperm unites with the mother's ovum (egg). At this instant a new human life is formed."

A related question, also answered differently by people of differing beliefs, is whether a developing fetus is a person. Several curricula offer as scientific fact moral or religious definitions of early fetuses as babies or people, in the process supplying inaccurate descriptions of their developmental state.

One curriculum that describes fetuses as "babies" describes the blastocyst, technically a ball of 107 to 256 cells at the beginning of uterine implantation, as "snuggling" into the uterus:

> After conception, the tiny baby moves down the fallopian tube toward the mother's uterus. About the sixth to tenth day after conception, when the baby is no bigger than this dot (.), baby snuggles into the soft nest in the lining of the mother's uterus.

Another teaches: "At 43 days, electrical brain wave patterns can be recorded, evidence that mental activity is taking place. This new life may be thought of as a thinking person." The curriculum cites a source which does not in fact call a 43-day-old fetus a "thinking person."

The same curriculum tells students: "Ten to Twelve Weeks After Conception: . . . He/she can hear and see." The curriculum cites a source that actually states, "Can the fetus see inside the uterus? We do not know." The source also states that fetuses begin to react to sounds between the fourth and fifth months, not at 10 to 12 weeks.

Gender Stereotypes

Many abstinence-only curricula begin with a detailed discussion of differences between boys and girls. Some of the differences presented are simply biological. Several of the curricula, however, present stereotypes as scientific fact.

• *Undermining girls' achievements.* Several curricula teach that girls care less about achievement and their futures than do boys.

One curriculum instructs: "Women gauge their happiness and judge their success by their relationships. Men's happiness and success hinge on their accomplishments." This curriculum also teaches:

> Men tend to be more tuned in to what is happening today and what needs to be done for a secure future. When women began to enter the work force at an equal pace with men, companies noticed that women were not as concerned about preparing for retirement. This stems from the priority men and women place on the past, present, and future.

Another curriculum lists "Financial Support" as one of the "5 Major Needs of Women," and "Domestic Support" as one of the "5 Major Needs of Men." The curriculum states:

Just as a woman needs to feel a man's devotion to her, a man has a primary need to feel a woman's admiration. To admire a man is to regard him with wonder, delight, and approval. A man feels admired when his unique characteristics and talents happily amaze her.

A third curriculum depicts emotions as limiting girls' ability to focus. It states: "Generally, guys are able to focus better on one activity at a time and may not connect feelings with actions. Girls access both sides of the brain at once, so they often experience feelings and emotions as part of every situation."

• *Girls as helpless and weak.* Some of the curricula describe girls as helpless or dependent upon men.

In a discussion of wedding traditions, one curriculum writes: "Tell the class that the Bride price is actually an honor to the bride. It says she is valuable to the groom and he is willing to give something valuable for her."

The curriculum also teaches: "The father gives the bride to the groom because he is the one man who has had the responsibility of protecting her throughout her life. He is now giving his daughter to the only other man who will take over this protective role.". . .

• *Reinforcing male sexual aggressiveness.* One curriculum teaches that men are sexually aggressive and lack deep emotions. In a chart of the top five women's and men's basic needs, the curriculum lists "sexual fulfillment" and "physical attractiveness" as two of the top five "needs" in the men's section. "Affection," "Conversation," "Honesty and Openness," and "Family Commitment" are listed only as women's needs. The curriculum teaches: "A male is usually less discriminating about those to whom he is sexually attracted. . . . Women usually have greater intuitive awareness of how to develop a loving relationship."

The same curriculum tells participants: "While a man needs little or no preparation for sex, a woman often needs hours of emotional and mental preparation.". . .

Several of the curricula that mention mental health concerns depict them as simple problems that can be fixed by abstaining from sexual activity. There does not appear to be scientific support for these assertions, however.

For example, one curriculum tells youth that a long list of personal problems—including isolation, jealousy, poverty, heartbreak, substance abuse, unstable long-term commitments, sexual violence, embarrassment, depression, personal disappointment, feelings of being used, loss of honesty, loneliness, and suicide—"can be eliminated by being abstinent until marriage." Other curricula teach that mental health problems are a consequence of sexual activity, without considering the evidence that these problems might themselves cause premature sexual activity, or that they might have a common origin.

Scientific Errors

In addition to the inaccurate and misleading information discussed above, a number of the abstinence-only curricula contain erroneous information about basic scientific facts. These errors cover a variety of issues:

• *Human genetics.* One curriculum states: "Twenty-four chromosomes from the mother and twenty-four chromosomes from the father join to create this new individual." In fact, human cells have 23 chromosomes from each parent, for a total of 46 in each body cell. The same curriculum also teaches: "Girls produce only female ovum, boys, however, have both male and female sperm." This too is inaccurate. Females produce ova with X chromosomes, and males produce sperm with either X or Y chromosomes. These combine to make an XX combination (female) or an XY combination (male). . . .

• *Puberty.* One curriculum tells instructors: "Reassure students that small lumps in breast tissue is common in both boys and girls during puberty. This condition is called gynecomastia and is a normal sign of hormonal changes." This definition is incorrect. In adolescent medicine, gynecomastia refers to a general increase in breast tissue in boys.

• *HIV.* Another curriculum erroneously includes "tears" and "sweat" in a column titled "At risk" for HIV transmission. In fact, according to the CDC, "[c]ontact with saliva, tears, or sweat has never been shown to result in transmission of HIV."

Under the Bush Administration, federal support for abstinence-only education has risen dramatically. This report finds that over two-thirds of abstinence-only education programs funded by the largest federal abstinence initiative are using curricula with multiple scientific and medical inaccuracies. These curricula contain misinformation about condoms, abortion, and basic scientific facts. They also blur religion and science and present gender stereotypes as fact.

"It is imperative that schools prepare students to survive the sexual aspect of life."

Safe-Sex Education Benefits Youths

Aaron Thomas Eske

In the following viewpoint Aaron Thomas Eske contends that schools should offer comprehensive sex education that teaches students about condoms, birth control, and sexual orientation as well as abstinence. Eske sees sex education as a kind of "survival course" that gives students all the information they need for whatever sexual choices they might make. Moreover, he argues, comprehensive sex education encourages safe sex but does not lead to increased sexual activity among teens. Eske was a student writer in Lincoln, Nebraska, when he wrote this essay.

As you read, consider the following questions:

1. What is the true purpose of school, in Eske's opinion?
2. According to the author, what percent of U.S. teenage suicides is related to sexual orientation?
3. In Eske's opinion, why is it ridiculous to believe that sex education programs might provoke teens to have sex?

Aaron Thomas Eske, "Schools Should Help Children Survive in the Real World," *SIECUS Report*, vol. 31, April/May 2003, pp. 17–18. Copyright © 2003 by the Sexuality Information and Education Council of the United States, Inc., 130 West 42nd St., Ste. 350, New York, NY 10036, www.siecus.org. Reproduced by permission.

Telling a 16-year-old boy or girl to abstain from sex is about as effective as stopping a moving train with your body. And telling every parent of a 16-year-old boy or girl to talk to their child about sex is about as effective as stopping a torpedo with your finger. Sadly, there are just some things in this world that won't happen, but luckily, schools can fill the gap.

Schools exist to prepare people for the future—to someday set foot on Mars or finally write the great American novel. Despite the thoughts that first come to mind, the majority of this preparation doesn't come from history textbooks or science experiments. The four core subjects are only the crust of a school's purpose while the true center is the all-consuming subject: *Survival 101.*

Without the hidden lessons in high school, I can definitively say that I would be a lesser person. I gained more from math than just the Pythagorean theorem. Solving algebra problems gave me the confidence that I would eventually need to make my own decisions, like where to apply to college and who to date. Psychology convinced me that my oddities and inner fears did not make me more crazy or different than any other high school student who felt the exact same things I did. And, lastly, while I certainly can't name half of the English books I read in those four years, I do remember each of the valuable ways of thinking they exposed me to. New experiences like a family of failed missionaries enduring the Congo in *The Poisonwood Bible,* and new perspectives like growing up gay in the 1950s from Paul Monette's *Becoming a Man* painted a new world that no one in my home could have possibly shown me, even if I hadn't been afraid to ask.

The "Ed" Courses

Even more important for me than the hidden lessons of high school were the messages that flashed like a neon light at 2 A.M. The dreaded classes that all ended in the abbreviation "ed" may have been a pain, but two years later I wish that college had an entire department dedicated to "ed" courses. In reality, students enrolled in "Career Ed," "Economics Ed," "Driver's Ed," and "Health Ed" with the same enthusiasm as a person making an appointment to have her wisdom teeth pulled. But we need these classes because they are more than just pains.

"Career Ed" helps us avoid a society full of garbage men by teaching students the difference between stocker and stalker on their resumes. "Economics Ed" helps us avoid a country that receives no federal taxes on April 16th. "Driver's Ed" helps us avoid a city plagued by fender-benders and crooked attempts at parallel parking. And "Health Ed" helps a person avoid spending his life sitting in a recliner with his head stuck in a bucket of fried chicken while a cigarette burns in the ashtray nearby. But better yet, "Health Ed" helps a mother avoid burying her 24-year-old son who died of AIDS or a teenage mother from dropping out of school.

The Value of Comprehensive Sex Education

Sex education needs to teach young people more than biology and risks. We need to know about contraceptives and places to go for help, too. We need to understand our own sexuality in order to better understand ourselves and the world around us. We need concrete education about sexuality and sexual expression so that we can look at the media and understand that it does not give us a realistic picture of sex. This is very important in our society today because the images the media portrays can be very harmful and misleading to youth.

We also need to learn how our sexuality affects others. We need to teach tolerance and understanding. In our increasingly ethnically diverse classrooms, we need to recognize the rights of others and ourselves. It is vital that sex education be provided to youth and that this education be complete.

Joni Meenagh, *SIECUS Report*, April/May 2003.

No one pretends that there aren't ignorant drivers on the roads that need some lessons. Why, then, do people pretend that there aren't ignorant people having sex that could benefit from a couple of safety classes? Alarmingly, high teen birth rates and HIV/STD infections are just as much a problem in America as car accidents, so why is there such a disparity in how these subjects are addressed? It's time for sex to stop being such a taboo. Otherwise, a problem will quickly evolve into a catastrophe far more threatening than any terrorist attack.

Schools Must Prepare Students

Imagine being Sally, who after waiting over a month for her period, takes a pregnancy test and a "plus" sign appears. Sally is 15 and is only one of a million teenagers a year in the United States to shake her head in disbelief at what she sees on the stick before her. Or imagine being Katy who tonight has the task of calling her boyfriend and telling him she just tested positive for HIV. Katy is three months away from graduating from high school and is only one of 27 to 54 teenagers a day in the United States who has to make a similar phone call. Or imagine being Gerry, who can't face the prospect of being ridiculed one more day at junior high about the "girly" way he talks. Gerry is 14 and is only one of nearly 30 percent of the total teenage suicides in the United States related to sexual orientation.

The presence of you and me on this planet is proof that sex exists just as much as job interviews and taxes. Therefore, it is imperative that schools prepare students to survive the sexual aspect of life with the same fervor they teach the difference between Newton's first and third laws of physics. It would be preposterous for a high school to only teach one of Newton's laws and not all three because they are all equally significant. The same argument should also be applied to teaching the many methods of contraception or protection. Yes, abstinence is an extremely valuable lesson, but it is still no more vital than how to properly put on a condom or what types of birth control options are available to teens.

A common fear among adults is that teaching students about sex encourages them to start having it. It is a fairly legitimate argument until you step back and see that a classroom discussion does not trigger a teenager's sex drive. A teen's hormones and desires already exist well before a condom demonstration, and anyone who says differently is severely kidding himself. The real result of sex education is an increase in safe sex and not a boost in sexual activity.

A similar concern among adults involves teaching students about homosexuality or gay sex. Some mothers believe that if little Johnny reads a book about two gay men falling in love that little Johnny will also want to fall in love with a man. And perhaps Johnny will someday, but not because the book changed him. Rather, because the book sorted out the confusion that already flooded his mind. Saying that a book can make someone gay is like suggesting that reading Richard Wright's *Black Boy* can make someone black.

Teaching Survival

Okay, so maybe sex education alone won't inspire a student to set his or her sights on becoming the President of the United States, but without it his or her dreams could easily be dashed. On a smaller scale, a comprehensive sex education program will help a future mother's dreams come true and ward off any potential STDs [sexually transmitted diseases] that threaten her reproductive system. Lastly, schools have the power to turn thousands of gay youth from being just another teen suicide statistic into being happy people able to achieve their dreams of love.

The main responsibility of schools is to teach survival, and in doing so, secure the dreams of America's children. Sadly, there are just some things in this world that ruin lives, but luckily, schools have a great opportunity to step in and grant some salvation.

4

| "*Is prioritising sexual 'openness' really doing young people any favours?*"

Safe-Sex Education Is Counterproductive

Alice O'Keeffe

Abstinence messages are probably the best way to protect teenagers from the dangers of early sexual experience, argues Alice O'Keeffe in the following viewpoint. The non-judgmental, "safe-sex" approach to sex education, which encourages sexual openness and contraceptive use, has actually led to an increase in sexual activity in younger teens, she points out. This is disquieting in nations like Britain, where the rates of teen pregnancy and sexually transmitted diseases have skyrocketed. She believes that a better approach to sex education might be progressive abstinence programs that emphasize self-esteem and discourage youths from seeking affirmation through sex. O'Keeffe is a writer for the British journal *New Statesman*.

As you read, consider the following questions:

1. What country has the highest teen pregnancy rate in Europe, according to O'Keeffe?
2. According to the author, condoms are ineffective against which sexually transmitted virus?
3. What percentage of British teens claim to have lost their virginity in a one-night stand, according to O'Keeffe?

Alice O'Keeffe, "Teenage Sex: Don't Scoff at Abstinence," *New Statesman*, vol. 132, November 2003, pp. 26–27. Copyright © 2003 by New Statesman, Ltd. Reproduced by permission.

Britain has never been a nation at ease with sex. Our Victorian forebears couldn't look at the legs of a piano without getting hot under the collar. Now, in the aftermath of the Sixties sexual revolution, we worry that things have gone too far, what with young holiday makers putting it about in Faliraki, footballers bragging about "roasting" young women and 18-year-olds getting jiggy in the Big Brother house. Are we ever going to get it right? Legislation won't put any self-respecting adolescent off "shagging" and, anyway, we're too progressive for that. All we can do is ply them with condoms and hope they don't get knocked up or stricken down with any love bugs.

In contrast, in the United States, chastity is all the rage. George Bush has created a $74m fund for sex education, available only to schools and groups that exclusively promote abstinence—contraception can be mentioned only in terms of its fallibility. In 35 per cent of all US school districts, sex education has been replaced with classes that focus solely on the abstinence-only approach. Funding for abstinence campaigns now outstrips safe-sex campaigns three-fold, with beneficiaries including the Silver Ring Thing, a faith-based organisation that encourages teenagers to purchase a $12 silver ring as a symbol of their commitment to remaining chaste until marriage. Abstinence movements now claim a membership of 2.5 million teenagers in the US.

The Non-Judgemental Approach

The idea of Bush defending the honour of his nation's daughters (pledgers are largely teenage girls) by bashing his Bible and flogging them cheap jewellery has provoked an understandably negative reaction from sexual health charities. Dr Kate Worsley, of Marie Stopes International, complains of the "focus on judgement" and neglect of "providing information and education to young people or helping them to make informed choices". Instead, Marie Stopes advocates a non-judgemental approach, offering "empowerment and negotiating skills" through discussion and information on contraception. Its "Like It Is" website for teenagers offers "everything you need to know about sex with no frills, no judgements, and definitely no holds barred". Careful to advocate contraception at every stage, it makes no attempt to talk down the joys of sex, offering only a brief caveat that "sex won't be perfect the first time".

Other liberal voices concur. "The focus on abstinence harkens a return to the dark ages," wrote Suzanne Goldenberg in the *Guardian* after visiting a Silver Ring Thing convention in the States. "Just say no to abstinence," cried Zoe Williams, lamenting the "bogus concepts of morality" of the chastity movement. Keep your moral repression, give us our hard-won sexual liberation, is the progressive consensus. But is prioritising sexual "openness" really doing young people any favours? A report from the House of Commons health committee in May [2003] warned that the country is experiencing a "crisis in sexual health". Britain has the highest rate of teenage pregnancy in Europe. Sexually transmitted diseases have risen to levels where the health service is unable to cope, with annual diagnoses of syphilis up 500 per cent and one in ten people aged 16–24 infected with chlamydia. Most sexual health clinics have waiting times of ten days for an appointment and, says the report, some are turning away hundreds of people a week. And though many infections are treatable with antibiotics, conditions such as pelvic inflammatory disease, which is often a result of untreated chlamydia, cause permanent internal damage and infertility. Those who have sex younger are much more likely to contract a sexually transmitted disease: among the under 16s, one in seven sexually active girls tests positive for chlamydia.

An Increase in Sexual Activity

The health committee explicitly attributes the rise in rates of infection to changing sexual behaviour in Britain. Any benefits of better education about and access to contraception are outweighed by the drop in the average age at which people first have sex, and the rise in the average number of partners. The 2001 National Survey of Sexual Attitudes and Lifestyles found that between 1990 and 2001 the average number of sexual partners increased from 8.6 to 12.7 for men and 3.7 to 6.5 for women, and that average age at first intercourse has fallen from 17 to 16. Although condom use is up, the overall figures for "high risk" sexual activity have also increased.

There are also strong arguments that even 100 per cent condom use would not be enough. Evidence is emerging that condoms do not protect from the human papilloma virus (HPV), which causes genital warts and cervical and anal cancer. Dr Trevor Stammers, a senior tutor at St George's Hospital, London, who has written extensively on sexual health, claims that sexual health campaigns have deliberately downplayed the fallibility of condoms on the basis that any doubts about their effectiveness would trigger a rise in HIV. "But HIV is the tip of the iceberg in terms of sexually transmitted diseases," he says. "AIDS is fatal, but so is HPV, and condoms offer no protection."

Abstinence—but Not Abstinence-Only

• [There is] widespread support for a strong abstinence message, but not for an abstinence-only message. Most adult and teen [survey] respondents said that abstinence is the first and best option for teens, but they also strongly believe that teens should be given information about contraception.

• Respondents believe teens should get more information about both abstinence and birth control rather than just one or the other.

• Americans reject the notion that stressing abstinence while providing information on contraception sends teens a confusing, mixed message.

• Sexually experienced teens wish they had waited.

• Teens generally express cautious attitudes toward early, casual sex.

State Health Watch, March 2003.

Even more controversial is a report . . . presented at a meeting in the House of Commons [in November 2003]. The research by Dr David Paton, professor of industrial economics at Nottingham University, has found a link between an increase in sexual health provision and rates of disease contraction—in other words, that the advice and access to contraception championed by those unwilling to appear moralistic about abstinence actually cause higher rates of disease. The Sexual Health of the Nation meeting will also examine how a campaign focusing on the reduction of casual sex, and not just wider access to contraception, has been responsible for success in fighting HIV in Uganda. Uganda has adopted what it calls the ABC approach to reducing HIV: "Abstain (from sex), Be Faithful (together), Condom Use (every time)." As a result, HIV rates dropped from 21 per cent to 9.8 per cent between 1991 and 1998.

Teens Are Not Resistant to Abstinence Messages

Not that sexual health is only about reducing rates of disease; the health committee report defines it as "a state of physical, emotional, mental and social well-being related to sexuality". Critics of abstinence argue that curiosity and exploration are a natural part of youth; a vision often not shared by surveyed teenagers. In the US, the Alan Guttmacher Institute found that 70 per cent of girls who had sex before the age of 16 regretted it, and one in five complained of physical coercion.

In a survey by the Institute of Education and University College London, 36 per cent of girls who had lost their virginity at 13 said they were "unhappy" about it, and 18 per cent said it "never should have happened". Early sex correlates positively with low socio-economic status, social exclusion and broken families. Dr Stammers, who has been teaching sex education in schools for more than ten years, says: "Most teenagers I have taught or talked to are not looking for sex, they're looking for love. I have sensitively discussed the idea of abstinence with classes of teenagers, listening to what they have to say, and they have on several occasions burst into applause when I finished. The resistance to the abstinence message does not come from the teenagers themselves."

Young people growing up in our consumer culture are not short of information about sex. It is all around them. They receive the message loud and clear that sex—preferably with a number of different partners—is an essential part of being a normal, happy person. We are not so good at being "open" about the reasons for waiting until you find someone you really desire and trust before becoming sexually active. One in three teenagers say they lost their virginity in a one-night stand, and only 15 per cent of boys cite "love and commitment" as their reason for first having sex. If, as these statistics suggest, teenagers have sex more from a sense of urgency than desire, and many subsequently feel unhappy about having done so, we need to ask where they will find any support for a positive alternative.

"I'm not sure how you would teach abstinence—the body of evidence shows it doesn't work," says Dr Worsley of Marie Stopes. "Abstinence messages conflict with all the other messages about sex which teenagers receive from the culture around them. And a cultural shift is very difficult to achieve."

Progressive Abstinence Programmes

The answer may indeed be to look to the United States—but to some progressive programmes that have been quietly revolutionising teenagers' sexual behaviour. Reva Klein, a journalist who has done extensive research into progressive education in the US and UK, emphasises that the most effective sex education programmes aim to build young people's self-esteem and "discourage them from seeking affirmation and escape through sexual relationships". She tells of one example of a "social and emotional development curriculum" in New Haven, Connecticut, where teenagers have been trained as peer educators and sex education classes are run without adults present. Within seven years, teenage pregnancy rates plummeted in this deprived urban area. Change is possible, she says, but we need to "tackle the root causes and take education much more seriously".

Education is undoubtedly where we must start. The problem extends far beyond the failings of traditional sex education. Teenagers—young, inexperienced and vulnerable to pressure—are left at the mercy of a culture which tells them that sex is the answer to everything. We must celebrate our prized sexual openness by using it to help them make positive decisions about when to start having sex. And maybe that decision will be to wait a while.

"It's not a question of teaching kids to approve of homosexuality. It's about teaching young people to respect people who are not like them."

Schools Should Promote Tolerance of Gay and Lesbian Students

Kevin Jennings and Kristen Loschert

Schools need to do more to create safe learning environments for lesbian, gay, bisexual, and transgendered (LGBT) students, argues Kevin Jennings in the following viewpoint. A high percentage of LGBT students encounter harassment, which can adversely affect their school performance and their educational aspirations, Jennings points out. The presence of student clubs such as the Gay-Straight Alliance and supportive faculty members can help to promote tolerance and curb anti-LGBT abuse, he maintains. Jennings is executive director of the Gay, Lesbian and Straight Education Network. He is interviewed by Kristen Loschert, a writer for *NEA Today* magazine.

As you read, consider the following questions:

1. What percentage of gay teens experience verbal abuse because of their sexual orientation, according to the viewpoint?
2. Why was Jennings harassed all through his junior high and high school years?
3. What is the average age of students who come out as lesbian, gay, bisexual, or transgendered, according to Jennings?

Kevin Jennings and Kristen Loschert, "Teaching Tolerance Is Academic," *NEA Today*, vol. 23, April 2003, pp. 34–35. Copyright © 2003 by the National Education Association of the United States. Reproduced by permission.

At a time when 84 percent of lesbian, gay, bisexual, and transgendered (LGBT) teens endure verbal abuse because of their sexual orientation and nearly 40 percent have been physically harassed, Kevin Jennings knows much work still must be done to create safe learning environments for all students. But as co-founder and executive director of the Gay, Lesbian and Straight Education Network (GLSEN), Jennings, a former history teacher, is working to ensure that "every child learns to value and respect all people, regardless of sexual orientation or gender identity." Through more than 2,500 high school clubs known as Gay-Straight Alliances, GLSEN empowers students and educators with the skills and resources they need to stop anti-LGBT bullying, work that earned Jennings an NEA [National Education Association] Human and Civil Rights award [in 2004]. Jennings speaks with *NEA Today*'s Kristen Loschert about the issues gay students face and ways educators can make a difference.

Enduring Harassment

Kristen Loschert: Why did you start GLSEN?

Kevin Jennings: I sort of came out in sixth grade, but like a lot of kids who get harassed for "being gay," it wasn't anything about my sexuality that prompted the harassment. It was because I was a boy who did his homework and paid attention in class and raised his hand and did all the things boys weren't supposed to do. I was harassed relentlessly through my junior high and high school years.

When I graduated from Harvard, I decided to become a teacher. I was pretty much forced out of my first job at a school in Providence, Rhode Island, because I was gay. And when I went to my second job I had a gay student who was really struggling. I saw how miserable he was and I saw how my own staying in the closet was kind of conveying to him a very damaging message that this is something to be ashamed of, something to hide.

I made a little promise to myself right there, and said, "I will do whatever I can so that the next generation has it better than we had it." So, I started GLSEN.

Have schools become any more accepting of gay educators?

Yes, I think things have improved. However, there's still a

lot of fear among a lot of gay people that they are going to be targeted unfairly if they go into professions that work with young people. There are only 14 states in which it's illegal to fire someone from their job because they're gay and only eight in which it's illegal to harass or discriminate against students because they are gay. So, while there's been more social acceptance, legally there is still an enormously long way to go before we have even basic protections in place.

Harassment at School Is the Rule, Not the Exception

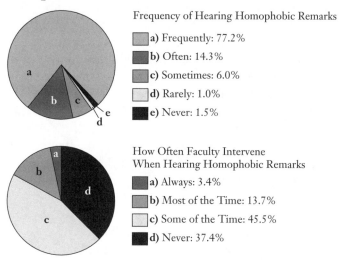

Frequency of Hearing Homophobic Remarks

a) Frequently: 77.2%

b) Often: 14.3%

c) Sometimes: 6.0%

d) Rarely: 1.0%

e) Never: 1.5%

How Often Faculty Intervene When Hearing Homophobic Remarks

a) Always: 3.4%

b) Most of the Time: 13.7%

c) Some of the Time: 45.5%

d) Never: 37.4%

Gay, Lesbian and Straight Education Network, 2003 National School Climate Survey, www.glsen.org.

Why has harassment of LGBT students been tolerated for so long?

Primarily because nobody has ever told young people it's wrong. And sadly, according to our National School Climate Survey, in 83 percent of cases where students are harassed because of their sexual orientation, teachers rarely or never intervene.

I'm not saying teachers are the problem. I'm saying the system does not prepare the teachers to succeed. If you don't give them the policy support, if you don't give them the training they need, you're really leaving them to their own devices. And that's a recipe for disaster.

The Need for Training

Are schools of education preparing future teachers to handle these issues?

We have found very few teacher education programs that address these issues in any way. And when they do, it is at the discretion of individual instructors and is not woven into the curriculum. So we continue to send teachers out there who have no training, trying to figure it out on their own.

At the same time, the average LGBT high school student comes out between 15 and 17. So they're coming out in school systems that have no more policies than they did when I was in high school, with teachers who have no more training. And then we're surprised when four out of five of these kids report that they routinely experience physical or verbal or sexual harassment. What did we think was going to happen?

Visibility is a mixed blessing. The great thing about visibility is yeah, now kids have gay-straight alliances. They know they're not alone. The bad thing is that when you're more visible, you're a bigger target.

Safer Learning Environments

How does the harassment affect students?

We know that students who are subjected to frequent harassment have demonstrably lower grade point averages— almost a full letter grade. We also know that they are much more likely to skip school. Over 31 percent of LGBT students have skipped at least one day of school in the past month because they are simply too afraid to go.

What can educators do to create safer learning environments for their LGBT students?

Supportive teachers make a big difference. When LGBT students know there's a teacher on their side, their grade point averages are a full letter grade higher. Meanwhile, those who do not have supportive teachers are two-and-a-half times more likely to say they don't plan to go to college.

When we polled teenagers to understand why they use homophobic language and what could get them to stop, 80 percent of girls and 68 percent of boys said that if a teacher they respected told them to stop using the language that would have a major impact on them. Teachers can make a huge difference. So, if you see something happening, do something. The worst thing to do is to say nothing because what you're doing is giving tacit permission for that behavior to continue.

On the proactive side, think about how you can work this into your classroom in age-appropriate and educationally appropriate ways. If you're teaching younger ages and putting together a unit on families, for example, acknowledge that some families have two moms or two dads.

It's not a question of teaching kids to approve of homosexuality. It's about teaching young people to respect people who are not like them, to teach students of different backgrounds and different value systems how to coexist in a respectful and peaceful way. That to me is just as essential as reading, writing, and arithmetic.

"Tolerance education and school-based clubs ignore the needs of heterosexual students [and] encourage questioning teens to embrace a gay identity."

Gay Tolerance Education Ignores the Needs of Straight Students

Joan Frawley Desmond

In the following viewpoint Joan Frawley Desmond questions the mind-set of tolerance educators who advocate for gay rights in public and private schools. While she recognizes the need to address the problem of antigay harassment in schools, Desmond argues that tolerance educators often force schools to adopt an agenda that includes a full-fledged acceptance of homosexuality. This agenda violates the rights of heterosexual students and parents who may believe that homosexuality is immoral or deviant, she concludes. Desmond has written for the *Wall Street Journal, First Things,* and the *National Catholic Register,* among other publications.

As you read, consider the following questions:

1. What kind of activities do Gay, Lesbian and Straight Education Network chapters plan for their members, according to Desmond?
2. Why was the author's godson upset with his instructors at an elite boarding school in New England?
3. What did a family life teacher tell Desmond's eighth-grade daughter and her classmates?

Joan Frawley Desmond, "(In)Tolerance Education," *Crisis,* vol. 23, February 2005, pp. 35–41. Copyright © 2005 by *Crisis.* Reproduced by permission.

U ntil a few years ago, the gay-rights movement kept its distance from my life in suburban California. I followed the movement's progress in the media and analyzed its claims in theology papers, but none of these matters directly intruded on my family's life and thus did not prompt any direct response. Then one morning, as I read the online bulletin issued by my son's Catholic high school, an item grabbed my attention: "We are announcing a new school club—'The Gay, Straight . . . and anything in between . . . Alliance' (GSA)!!" I read over the announcement several times, pondering the oddly jocular tone of the words, "and anything in between." I spent the rest of the morning reviewing the GSA network's significant Internet presence and crafting an e-mail to the club's adviser. Additional e-mails, a meeting with the adviser, communication with the headmaster, and, finally, a letter to the local bishop led to the short-lived closing of the group on orders from the diocese.

The tug-of-war with the school over the GSA club led me to explore the increasing clout of the gay-rights movement in American schools and to grapple with the problems posed by "tolerance" education and affiliated support groups. Our society rightly seeks to end the harassment of homosexual students in schools that have witnessed a decline in civility and a rise in crude behavior. And as many parents and teachers will attest, the stigma of homosexuality remains strong in an adolescent population that struggles to project normalcy during a vulnerable time.

An Unjust Solution

Nevertheless, we're in real danger of broadly adopting an unjust solution to the stigmatization of gay students that will harm many more young people than it will help. Designed explicitly to protect marginalized students and implicitly to enforce acceptance of "sexual differences," tolerance education and school-based clubs ignore the needs of heterosexual students, encourage questioning teens to embrace a gay identity, and violate the rights of teachers and parents who resist this current. Meanwhile, the appearance of these clubs in religious schools generates unnecessary confusion about Christian teaching on marriage and human sexuality.

Advocating the inclusion of gay and lesbian students as a civil rights matter, tolerance education and support groups such as the GSA club at my son's school provide an empathetic forum for the concerns of sexual minorities. Once established, though, the agenda usually broadens considerably—particularly in liberal, urban schools on the East and West coasts. While addressing the genuine problem of anti-gay harassment, student and faculty activists also seek greater institutional accommodation within a stubbornly heterosexual school culture. Early on, GSAs made headlines when members successfully negotiated the right of same-sex couples to attend proms. Equity in public displays of affection followed. Gay pride events and a "Day of Silence"—an annual protest designed to underscore the emotional costs of gay self-censorship—have surfaced in more than a thousand schools nationwide. Now, advocates for "safe schools" are shifting their focus to "transgender students," and groups have begun to lobby for separate bathrooms for cross-dressers.

Confusion About Human Sexuality

Even 20 years ago, GSAs and other elements of tolerance education would have prompted more resistance in our schools. Today, while the movement still provokes controversy, its steadily increasing role in shaping American school culture reveals a growing level of confusion regarding the entire subject of human sexuality. Forty years after the onset of the sexual revolution, students and teachers are grappling with a breakdown in the transmission of practical, moral, and religious principles and rituals that once helped the young anticipate the achievement of adulthood through the gateway of marriage and family life. The transparent, sequenced steps of courtship are long gone, for example. No one still expects administrators, teachers, and parents to reach a consensus on proper teenage behavior. Tolerance education flourishes in the incoherence that remains.

This approach must be anchored in a rich, systematic teaching on the intrinsic dignity of each student, and an exploration of the deeper purpose of human sexual identity and expression. There also must be an engagement of individualistic, utilitarian values that lead the young both to resist any constraints imposed on their freedom and to fear the sacrifices real love requires. For this reason, it would be shortsighted to plan a response that simply targets the clubs for elimination. Any effective strategy must go to the heart of the matter: a recovery of fidelity to the truth about the human person, his intrinsic dignity, and the purpose of human sexuality.

A Quiet Infiltration

While the Golden State may well be a predictable beach-head for gay rights advocacy in schools, tolerance education, often in the form of GSA clubs allied with GLSEN (Gay, Lesbian and Straight Education Network) chapters—and those with similar titles and missions—can be found in public and elite private schools, religious and secular, throughout the country.

An Offensive Assertion

When harassment based on sexual orientation is explicitly banned, school staff and students are inevitably trained that the *reason* that such harassment is wrong is not because all harassment is wrong or because all people should be treated with respect, but because *"there is nothing wrong with being gay or lesbian."* Such an assertion is not only offensive to the moral standards of most Americans and to the historical teachings of most major religions, but it flies in the face of hard scientific data showing the high rates of promiscuity, physical disease, mental illness, substance abuse, child sexual abuse, and domestic violence that result from homosexual behavior.

Peter Sprigg, congressional testimony, February 19, 2003.

Since the first GSA clubs surfaced in the late 1980s, their central purpose has remained unchanged: to establish "safe schools" for gay and lesbian students and to combat "homophobia." What continues to shift is just how activists define these goals. A sampling of GLSEN's glossary of relevant terms hints at the movement's evolving points of reference:

• *Queer:* Historically negative term used against people perceived to be LGBT, "queer" has more recently been reclaimed by some people as a positive term describing all those who do not conform to rigid notions of gender and sexuality. Queer is often used in political context and in academic settings to challenge traditional ideas about identity ("queer theory").

• *Heterosexism:* Bias against non-heterosexuals based on a belief in the superiority of heterosexuality. Heterosexism does not imply the same fear and hatred as homophobia. It can describe seemingly innocent statements, such as "She'd drive any man wild," based on the assumption that heterosexuality is the norm.

GLSEN chapters organize members for gay pride marches, produce curricula attacking "heterosexism," oppose legislation banning gay marriage, and back civil suits that mandate GLSEN-sponsored sensitivity training for students and teachers. Some GLSEN training materials merely stress the need to protect gay and lesbian students, citing high dropout rates among victimized groups. But other curricula push harder: Teachers must not articulate preconceived notions regarding gender identity and sexual orientation in classroom discussions, lest they find themselves in the crosshairs of GLSEN and the American Civil Liberties Union (ACLU). . . .

Ham-Handed Advocacy

Publicly, tolerance proponents often articulate a "live and let live" philosophy. But the movement's mindset is too intrusive to be confused with such a libertarian position. If we celebrate moral relativism as creative and valuable, then we must reject an adherence to moral norms as rigid and homophobic. If we applaud the courage of those who test sexual boundaries, then we must diminish those who don't push the envelope.

An example of this dynamic is spelled out by my godson, who studies at an elite Episcopal boarding school in New England. His school doesn't offer a single course on chastity education, but he is required to watch a film on gay, bisexual, and transgender people. After showing the film, his instructors demand not tolerance but affirmation from the assembled students. "In the discussions," he writes me, with a touch of anger, "we were expected to agree with everything the movie said or be scorned by the faculty as 'homophobic.' We watched the movie as if the people in it were supposed to be our role models."

Ham-handed advocacy masked as education antagonizes many adolescents like my godson. Ultimately, though, the aggressive exposure of sexual deviancy may do real harm, desensitizing teens and lowering their standards of behavior in heterosexual relationships. Further, no one is helping my godson with the critical task that lies ahead: the shift from adolescent preoccupations to a deeper understanding of his own sexuality. Will he learn to embrace masculinity as a gift that finds its true expression in the faithful, fruitful, and permanent bonds of married love? . . .

Normalizing Disorder

Our family recently moved from California to the Washington, D.C., area. Nevertheless, we continue to confront the growing impact of the tolerance movement. My daughter's family life teacher brightly informs the assembled eighth-grade girls, "Some of you will be attracted to men, and some of you will be attracted to women!" At another time in this convent school's past, the reverend mother offered starkly different categories that shaped the students' vision of the future: "Some of you will marry, and some of you will be called to the celibate life." Our central identity as children of a loving God, made in His image, fuels the discernment of our earthly vocation. Yet, if we're not careful, the gay identity movement will succeed in convincing its members—and the rest of us, too—that sexual orientation trumps everything. They would have us believe that homosexual and heterosexual persons operate in two distinct worlds, with God's moral law, His redeeming love, and His saving grace only operative within the latter sphere. . . .

The morphing of diversity education into gay-rights advocacy might be dismissed as yet another harmless educational fad if the potential for danger weren't so great. A deception is being perpetrated. Vulnerable adolescents are offered "an entire package of new ideas and concepts about sex, gender, human relationships, anatomical relationships, and personal destiny," psychotherapist and author Joseph Nicolosi observes. Christian leaders and educators—particularly the Catholic bishops—must engage the underlying misconceptions that fuel this movement's growth. And they must stop it.

Periodical Bibliography

The following articles have been selected to supplement the diverse views presented in this chapter.

Mary Jo Anderson	"Suffer the Children," *Crisis*, April 2004.
Joanne Csete	"Abstinence and Ignorance," *Human Rights*, Fall 2004.
Gina Dalfonzo	"Real Sex-Ed Polls," *American Enterprise*, September 2003.
Daisy Hernandez	"Young and Out: Anything but Safe," *ColorLines*, Winter 2004–2005.
Kenneth Jost	"Gays on Campus," *CQ Researcher*, October 1, 2004.
John Leo	"Sex for Dummies," *U.S. News & World Report*, May 23, 2005.
LeeChe Leong	"Virulent Virginity," *ColorLines*, Winter 2004–2005.
Joni Meenagh	"Sex Education Must Teach More than Biology, Risks," *SIECUS Report*, April/May 2003.
Ben Shapiro	"The Radical Homosexual Agenda," *Conservative Chronicle*, March 16, 2005.
Erica Smiley	"Your Health Choice," *Political Affairs*, March 2003.
Sarah Sparks	"Study Casts New Doubt on Abstinence-Only Approach," *Education Daily*, February 4, 2005.
State Health Watch	"Just Don't Do It," March 2003.
Cal Thomas	"Facts Do Not Support Sex Educators," *Conservative Chronicle*, March 16, 2005.
Steve Yoder	"Distortion 101," *In These Times*, February 28, 2005.

CHAPTER 4

Are Some Sexual Behaviors Unacceptable?

Chapter Preface

In 1995 John Robin Sharpe, a retired city planner from Vancouver, British Columbia, was charged with possession of child pornography. Sharpe had collected photographs, books, and stories depicting minors engaging in sexual activity; he had also created such pornographic writings and drawings for his own personal use. Sharpe's case resulted in a controversial ruling in the year 2000 in which the Canadian Supreme Court upheld previous laws banning the possession, making, and distribution of pornography involving actual children. The court also decided, however, that stories, drawings, or paintings depicting sex with children were not illegal as long as they were created by an individual for his or her own private use.

The issue is undeniably troubling and challenging. On the one hand, laws banning child pornography are largely designed to protect children from sexual exploitation and abuse. In addition, many experts agree that pedophiles can be incited to sexually abuse youths by viewing pornographic images involving children. But analysts continue to disagree about the banning of images that *appear to be* children engaging in sexual conduct but that do not involve real children. The advent of modern computer image-enhancing technology, which can create virtual pictures that look very real, complicates this debate.

In 1996 the U.S. Congress stepped into the debate over virtual child porn by adding a provision to the Child Pornography Protection Act (CPPA). This new provision held that possessing or distributing a visual image that "conveys the impression" of a minor engaging in sexual acts was a crime. According to Congress, pedophiles use such images to arouse themselves and to lure children into sexual activities; some representatives also argued that virtual child porn can "desensitize the viewer to the pathology of sexual abuse or exploitation of children." The law was challenged, however, by several anticensorship groups, who contended that the banning of virtual images violated the First Amendment's protection of freedom of expression. As Joan Bertin of the National Coalition Against Censorship stated, "Congress is saying that it is criminal even to think repulsive thoughts, and that's a huge problem." Ultimately, the debate was taken to the U.S. Supreme Court, which struck down the CPPA's ban on virtual child porn. Speaking for the majority, Justice Anthony Kennedy wrote, "The argument that virtual child pornography whets pedophiles' appetites and encourages them to engage in illegal conduct is unavailing because the mere tendency of speech to encourage unlawful acts is not a sufficient reason for banning it . . . absent some showing of a direct connection between the speech and the imminent illegal conduct."

As these debates over the legality of virtual child pornography suggest, the line separating personal tastes and behaviors from dangerous or socially unacceptable actions can be difficult to draw. In the following chapter authors further examine the acceptability of controversial sexual practices as they discuss pornography, prostitution, and polyamorous relationships.

"Considerable harm can come from long-term porn abuse."

Pornography Is Harmful

Rebecca Hagelin

Rebecca Hagelin is director of communications and public relations at the Heritage Foundation in Washington, D.C. In the following viewpoint Hagelin maintains that the United States is experiencing a disturbing increase in the availability of pornography. This proliferation of pornography is damaging family relationships, raising crime rates, and causing an increase in sex addiction, Hagelin writes. Most disturbingly, a majority of child molesters habitually use pornography, and youths are at increased risk of encountering pornography and sexual predators on the Internet.

As you read, consider the following questions:
1. How much money do Americans spend on pornography each year, according to Hagelin?
2. According to the author, in what way is President Clinton to blame for the recent increase of pornography in the United States?
3. What are the four stages of porn abuse that lead to sexual addiction, according to Hagelin?

Rebecca Hagelin, "Overdosing on Porn," *World & I*, vol. 19, March 2004, p. 20. Copyright © 2004 by News World Communications, Inc. Reproduced by permission.

Recently, the availability of pornography has exploded, particularly on the Internet. Today, 1,000 U.S.-based firms operate more than 100,000 subscription porn Web sites.

Back in November [2003], *60 Minutes* aired a piece by Steve Kroft on the mainstreaming of the pornography industry. He attended a porn trade show, talked with porn stars and those who market their work, exposed the companies of surprisingly high stature that now profit from smut, and explored just how pervasive the industry has become.

The venerable CBS news magazine jumped from twenty-first in ratings to second the week Kroft's report appeared. America, it seems, just can't get enough porn.

A Booming Business

From the Internet, with its a la carte offerings of porn for every pervert; to the hotel/motel industry, which does a tidy business selling in-room blue movies to guests; to the video industry, with its massive Hollywood-like studios; to the stores trafficking in adult films that are cropping up in almost every community in America, porn—which seemed to be dying a slow death as recently as 15 years ago—has become a booming business.

Consider: Sex is the No. 1 topic searched for on the Internet. Gambling is second.

Americans spend $10 billion per year on porn, as much as they spend on sporting events, movies, or music. Paul Fishbein, founder and president of *Adult Video News* magazine and promoter of the show Kroft attended, said there are 800 million rentals each year of adult videotapes and DVDs.

The industry has responded by churning out 11,000 movies per year, according to Kroft's report. That's up from 1,000 a decade ago, according to Holman Jenkins, a columnist and editorial board member of the *Wall Street Journal*, who has written widely on the issue. Bill Lyon, a lobbyist, told *60 Minutes* that the porn industry employs 12,000 people in California and pays the state $36 million in taxes per year.

A Rising Tide of Porn

Literature that could be classified as hard-core porn has existed for centuries, and hard-core porn movies have been around almost as long as film itself. According to Ed Halter, writing for the *Village Voice*, today's stars with porn in their past, such as Pamela Lee Anderson, Paris Hilton, and Rob Lowe, are following a trail blazed by, among others, Joan Crawford, Marilyn Monroe, and Chuck Connors.

Sexually Stunted

Sandy Bentley, the *Playboy* cover girl and former [Hugh] Hefner girlfriend (along with her twin sister Mandy), describes Hefner's current sexual practices in just enough detail to give you a good long pause:

"The heterosexual icon [Hugh Hefner] . . . had trouble finding satisfaction through intercourse; instead, he liked the girls to pleasure each other while he masturbated and watched gay porn."

This statement may seem either shocking or trivial. But it points to that which Hefner's detractors have been saying for years: Pornography stifles the development of genuine human relationships. Pornography is a manifestation of arrested development. Pornography reduces spiritual desire to Newtonian mechanics. Pornography, indulged long enough, hollows out sex to the point where even the horniest old goat is unable to physically enjoy the bodies of nubile young females.

Read Mercer Schuchardt, *Christianity Today*, December 2003.

But in recent years, porn availability has exploded, particularly on the Internet. Today, 1,000 U.S.-based firms operate more than 100,000 subscription porn Web sites. Two-thirds do not even warn about their adult content, and only 3 percent require viewers to prove they are adults before entering. Three in five searches conducted on the Net in the United States are to seek out porn, according to a study published in the *Washington Times*.

Child porn—which is illegal to create worldwide—continues to grow as well. The FBI pursued about 700 cases of child porn in 1998; by 2001, it was pursuing more than 2,800. Demand for pornographic images of babies and toddlers is soaring, according to Professor Max Taylor, who has documented efforts to fight pedophilia information networks in Europe. Approximately 20 new children and 20,000 new images of child porn are posted to the Internet each week, experts have said.

The U.S. Customs Service estimates that 100,000 Web sites offer child pornography worldwide; more than half of them originate in the United States. N2H2 (www.n2h2.com), a Seattle-based firm that sells Internet filters, reports that 403 child porn sites appeared in the five-month period from April to September 2000 and that 231 per month appeared from February to July 2001.

As the numbers have grown, so has the variety of acts depicted in these movies. Virtually every imaginable fetish is addressed. As Dennis Hof, an associate of *Hustler* magazine publisher Larry Flynt, told the *New York Observer*, "You've got Larry and [*Penthouse* publisher Bob] Guccione doing things that 10 years ago you'd go to prison for. Then you've got all this Internet stuff—dogs, horses, 12-year-old girls, all this crazed Third-World s— going on."

Who Is to Blame?

How did this happen? How did the number of movies produced each year increase tenfold in a decade? How did such mainstream companies as Hilton and Marriott, General Motors and Time Warner become leading—although not proud (don't, for instance, look for listings of the porn profits in their annual reports)—purveyors of smut? According to Jenkins, this is one case where we legitimately can blame President Clinton—at least to some extent.

When Clinton took office, he fired all the sitting U.S. attorneys, which destroyed a bevy of prosecutions. He told their replacements to focus on child porn and used his bully pulpit to condemn violence in movies, rather than sex. As a result, no federal prosecutor pressed an obscenity case for 10 years.

U.S. Attorney Mary Beth Buchanan of Los Angeles broke the streak only recently when she filed charges against Extreme Associates, whom officials have characterized as one of the most blatant violators of federal obscenity laws. "Federal prosecution of obscenity crimes is like using a dump truck to pick up waste and filth instead of a spoon," said Dan Panetti, vice president for legal and public policy for the National Coalition Against Pornography. "It is the appropriate tool to enforce community standards and, in its absence for the past 10 years, the hard-core pornographers have flooded our culture with a cesspool of prosecutable material."

The industry took its measure of President Clinton and his message—that government was backing away from obscenity enforcement—and took advantage. It adapted to the Internet, learned to find and market stars, and attracted venture capital from Wall Street and long-term investment from some of the nation's leading corporations.

Enormously Profitable

The reason is simple: Despite all the new players in the market, porn remains enormously profitable. Because of the social stigma that continues to accrue to porn—the factor that drove up the ratings for *60 Minutes*—demand outstrips supply, customers want their purchases kept secret (American Express has ceased to process transactions for porn services because of the number of customers who claim they didn't purchase the porn items listed on their statements), and markup remains extremely high.

According to the *60 Minutes* report, DirecTV, owned by Hughes Electronics, a subsidiary of General Motors, pulled in $500 million from adult entertainment [in 2003]. Comcast, the nation's largest cable company, made $50 million. All the nation's top cable operators—from Time Warner to Cablevision—distribute sexually explicit material.

To the nation's top hotel chains—Hilton, Marriott, Hyatt, Sheraton, and Holiday Inn—smut can mean the difference between red and black ink on the ledger. The *60 Minutes* report said that half the guests in these hotels order in-room adult movies and that these orders account for nearly 70 percent of their profits.

It's probably not possible to expect things to return to the days of President Reagan, whose attorney general, Edwin Meese, headed a commission that looked into pornography, its effects on Americans, and how it could be slowed. The question today becomes: What can we expect as porn becomes more accepted throughout society?

Calculating the Damage

It is now clear that considerable harm can come from long-term porn abuse. In just the last five years, organizations have proliferated to help people who feel a compulsive "addiction" to pornography. Pornography by itself—not as part of an accusation of adultery—has begun to arise with what Jenkins calls "alarming frequency" in divorce and custody proceedings.

That's not to mention the Harvard Divinity School dean, Disney Internet executive, dozens of *New York Times* employees, countless college professors and schoolteachers, and other once-reputable citizens in communities from coast to coast who have been disgraced, arrested, or fired because of the discovery of porn on their home or office computers.

"The more accessible the material, the larger number of people who will be willing to consume it because they can do so discreetly," Jenkins said in a February 2001 article for *Policy Review* magazine. "The larger and more scalable the market, the more it can supply material to dovetail with every individual quirk or taste. Given the way porn seems to act on those who are most susceptible to it, we may be surprised at the results."

Jenkins pointed to Dr. Mark Laaser, a cofounder of the Christian Alliance for Sexual Recovery and himself a recovering sex addict. Citing recent research, Laaser says just as alcoholics build up tolerance and must then drink more to receive the same effect, sex addicts—because of naturally occurring chemicals in the brain—also build up tolerance and need more input for the same satisfaction. The National Council on Sexual Addiction Compulsivity estimates that 6 to 8 percent of Americans are sex addicts. "I have treated [more than] 1,000 male and female sex addicts," Laaser told Congress in 2002. "Almost all of them began with pornography."

Sex Addiction

They start with pornography and move through four stages to sexual addiction, according to Dr. Victor Cline, an expert on the topic. They begin by using porn as an aphrodisiac. From that, they move to escalation, in which they require more explicit and deviant material to meet their needs. As this progresses, a third stage—desensitization—takes hold, as material that once was perceived as gross, shocking, and disturbing becomes common and acceptable.

Finally, some begin to act out the behaviors viewed in pornography, which leads, for men, to a dehumanization of the women in their lives. This partially explains why Phoenix police found that neighborhoods where adult businesses were located had a 43 percent higher rate of property crimes and a 4 percent higher rate of violent crimes. It almost fully explains the 506 percent increase in sex crimes.

For these men, sexual gratification begins to overwhelm all other desires. According to the National Coalition Against Pornography (NCAP), they come to view sex solely as a vehicle for their own physical pleasure. They come to see it as an act without consequence with a person who doesn't matter, and they view marriage and sound relationships as barriers to happiness. This leads to breakdowns in relationships and often divorce, according to information from the NCAP.

Pornography's Fruits

Porn drives some to engage in behaviors they previously had managed to hold in check. For instance, in a study of convicted child molesters, 77 percent of those who molested boys and 87 percent of those who molested girls admitted to the habitual use of pornography in the commission of their crimes. They use porn to stimulate themselves and break down the inhibitions of children.

Thankfully, nearly all children are reluctant to take part in such activities. They don't understand—as an adult would—why this touching is improper. But they know it is; they recoil when it happens, and they're never again comfortable around that adult. This is why experts on child sex abuse and porn invariably tell parents to pay attention when their children are wary of a particular adult.

The Internet not only brings porn into the home, where people can view it in private; it removes the age restriction. As a result, 9 out of 10 children ages 8 to 16 who have Internet access have viewed porn Web sites, usually while looking up information for homework assignments, according to a study by the London School of Economics.

With the Web, it's not just porn sites that present a problem; it's email as well. Stories of adults who lured children into porn or simple sexual abuse through the Internet are too numerous to mention. A "friend" appears in an otherwise harmless chat room. A relationship forms. A meeting is arranged.

This is where the problem gets huge. A survey for the Kaiser Family Foundation found that 90 percent of teens and young adults have access to email, and half check their in-box at least once a day. Three out of four have access at home, and nearly one in three can access email from their own rooms, unsupervised by parents.

Children on the Web have a one in five chance of being approached via email by a sexual predator, and one in 33 receive aggressive solicitation, such as phone calls, mail, money, or gifts. Some 40 percent of the people charged with child pornography also sexually abuse children, according to a Reuters news service story. . . . In nearly 9 in 10 cases, predators went into chat rooms or began an instant messaging conversation with their intended victims.

A recent study by the University of Pennsylvania indicates that 345,000 children 17 or younger are prostitutes or performers in porn movies. Who knows how many may have gotten their start participating in what they thought were innocent chat rooms?

Unacceptable Costs

Lyon, the industry lobbyist, likes to talk about the profits involved and the business acumen of the proprietors. "I was rather shocked," he says, "to find that these are pretty bright businesspeople who are in it to make a profit. And that's what it's all about."

Actually, that's not what it's all about. There are lots of profits in the illegal drug trade, too, but we don't condone it because we know that it's not a victimless crime. As the evidence piles up that this open door to pornography also brings about more victims and victimization, will we react similarly? Will we see that these profits—like drug profits—come at an unacceptable cost to society? More important, will we see this before it's too late?

"Many therapists say they see no harm [in pornography] for either sex as long as it doesn't become a compulsion."

Pornography Is Not Harmful

Part I: Manny Howard; Part II: Michelle Quinn

The authors of the following two-part viewpoint maintain that pornography is generally a harmless form of entertainment for adults. In Part I, New York–based writer Manny Howard contends that most American men look at pornography, including Internet porn sites, on a regular basis. In Part II, Michelle Quinn, a writer for the *San Jose Mercury News*, reports that a growing number of women are purchasing pornography and erotica. Increasingly, she notes, women are able to avoid degrading or offensive porn videos by selecting pornographic movies directed by women.

As you read, consider the following questions:

1. Why does Howard prefer to pay for online pornography rather than surf the Internet for free porn?
2. What is spurring women's increased interest in pornography, according to Quinn?
3. According to Harrison Voight, quoted by Quinn, what is the difference between erotica and pornography?

I

There is a moment in every marriage when husband and wife look into each other's eyes and acknowledge that they don't know quite as much about each other as they thought—and that now, they know more than they maybe care to.

Upstairs, the kids were tucked in their cribs and sleeping soundly. I diced vegetables for dinner and rambled idly about the minor triumphs and disappointments of my workday. My wife, Lisa, half-listened while working through our mountain of bills, all the while making sympathetic noises at what were, by and large, the appropriate moments. And then there was a pause in our patter.

A Crossroad

"What is this charge, 'Suze Randall Photo'?" Lisa asked as she looked at the credit card bill. "It's for $29.95, and this is the second month in a row I've seen the charge."

Recognizing a crossroad, I stopped chopping the vegetables. Lisa had asked me a very straightforward question. Therefore, I reasoned that it deserved an equally straightforward answer. This did not calm the spasm that had taken charge of my gut, however.

"Oh, that? That is a subscription for an Internet porn site," I said as matter-of-factly as any grown man, any father of two, could manage after being suddenly transformed in his wife's eyes into a breast-obsessed pubescent.

"Oh," said Lisa, her eyes dropping from mine to the paper in her hand. "$29.95 every month?"

"That's not that bad," I said with mock cheer in my voice, returning to my dicing and what passed as semiregular breathing, explaining, "some sites cost as much as 39, 40 bucks."

The learning curve was steep, but Lisa, true to form, made the ascent in alarmingly good time. She had just discovered the existence of monthly subscriptions to pornographic Websites. She had learned that her husband was one such subscriber. She was no longer confused, she was also not exactly angry. Neither was she particularly chatty during dinner.

At the risk of shocking some of the more naive wives in

the room, let me just say that it's a given that pornography is a central part of an American man's life. The thing is, most men are just less clumsy than I am. During a night out with the boys, as I merrily relayed the story of my deep embarrassment to the fellahs over beers at our local bar, they all begged to know why I hadn't just lied. I won't say I was not tempted, but it was my considered opinion that Lisa knew perfectly well what "Suze Randall Photo" was likely to be—or could guess. It made no sense to both get busted with my hands in my trousers and caught in a lie about my hands in my trousers.

It's not like I'm not attracted to my wife—Lisa is both incredibly hot and incredibly cool. If she told me I could never view porn again, I would do what she said. But luckily, Lisa's politics do not incorporate a reflexive loathing of pornography as an attack on womankind. I suppose Lisa sees pornography as an outlet, not evil, not ideal, but necessary, somehow. Nonetheless, she reminded me that we were working to pare down the balance of that particular charge card, and she would prefer to have Suze's episodic charge removed from it. I said that that would be easy enough to do, and we said nothing else about the episode.

I, unfortunately, chose to misread her calm reaction as a tacit acceptance, which prompted me to neglect her request to remove or even redirect the charge. A month went by without incident and I forgot all about my promise—that is, until two months later, when Lisa stormed into our study, stabbing the air with a credit card bill.

"I thought that we'd agreed," she barked. "This is the third month in a row. It's the only charge on that account, and I'm sick of looking at your and Suze's porno bill!"

I stammered stupidly, said something about having been too busy, but it was worse than hopeless. This was going to hurt. "Suze" was a person in Lisa's mind now. A virtual lover? Lord, I hoped not.

The next morning I canceled the subscription outright.

A Conversation About Pornography

When tempers had calmed and I had assured Lisa that Suze had been banished from the card, we had a conversation about pornography. She asked why I needed to subscribe to sites. My best guess was that what is different is good. I also explained that surfing for free porn (and there is plenty of it) puts you up close and personal with too many sites described as "teen," and that, as a new dad, I could not bear the notion. Subscribing to adult sites guaranteed much more control of the content.

We left it at that.

Not that I kicked the habit completely. Soon I moved on to other sites and charged them on busier cards, hoping Lisa wouldn't notice. And for a while, she didn't.

Then one evening I noticed that my computer was on, and my Web browser open . . . on the screen right next to what I had believed was a thoroughly well-buried folder in my "favorites" list. I will not repeat the titles of the sites now, but they leave very little to the imagination.

For men, the term "personal computer" has an unintended but central second meaning. I don't know a married man who is not paralyzed with fear whenever he is asked, innocently enough, by his wife if she could please use his computer to log on to the Web to check e-mail or shop. One's computer, especially one's browser, is a deeply personal space—horribly autobiographical and, often, deeply revealing. If it were up to me, the personal computer would remain just that, and be strictly a "his" and "hers" appliance.

A Sexaholic?

I went down to dinner prepared for the worst. Lisa had, she explained over dessert, logged on to my computer, and for some still unknowable reason, my computer had voluntarily coughed up the homepage for every porn site I had ever thought enough of to keep.

Lisa said the deluge was entirely overwhelming, and that it took forever to clear the pages just so she could log on to a hardware website.

She was embarrassed to have been caught snooping (if involuntarily, to hear her tell it). Nonetheless, she was concerned. I assured her that I was not subscribing to more than two sites (a lie—I presently subscribe to three). I said that I was embarrassed also, and didn't know what to say to make her feel better. Generously, she chalked this second episode up to bad timing and shrugged it off, but the conversation continued after we both retired to the porch for a big cocktail.

At lunch the next day with an old friend I relayed this second episode, confiding that Lisa was now concerned that I might be a sexaholic. "A sexaholic? 'Cause of a few dozen porn sites in your favorites list?" he laughed. "You and the rest of the men in America."

II

Alone at home at the end of a hard day, a woman takes a moment from her endless responsibilities to savor a moment of peace and quiet.

And pops in a porn video.

Thanks to the Internet, mail-order video and DVD rental outlets, plus a general shift in sexual mores, a small but growing number of women are turning up the heat in their sex lives by turning to erotica and pornography.

Adult video and toy stores are catering to women with clean, well-lighted places to peruse sexual material and products geared for their enjoyment. Books such as *The Ultimate Guide to Adult Videos* . . . are aimed at pornography neophytes, especially women, says Chris Fox, publicity coordinator at Cleis [Press]. "People don't think of women as porn consumers."

Still Taboo

And why should they? For many, women buying and watching pornography is still taboo. The mere idea questions assumptions about women's sexuality: that women aren't visually stimulated. That women prefer bodice-ripper romance novels to explicit videos and pornographic photos. That women feel it's immoral or anti-feminist to buy and watch pornography.

Psychologists, sex researchers and those who sell pornography say women's interest in pornography has been spurred by changes in contemporary culture, from the privacy afforded by the Internet to the trendiness of sex in TV's *Sex and the City* and other mainstream entertainment.

"Women are more comfortable about sexuality," says

Lonnie Barbach, psychologist and author of many books, including the 1975 how-to-become-orgasmic classic *For Yourself*. "Every year, the culture gets more open."

Society's Negative Attitude About Pornography

Pornography is not ugly; our society's attitudes about sex are ugly. Pornography does not degrade the people in it; our society degrades people for desiring sex. Pornography is not shameful to enjoy; our society says we do not deserve the exquisite pleasure and joy that comes from "coming." Pornography is powerful because it dares. Dares to shamelessly expose that which has been kept hidden, dares to give form to nameless desires. Shows life after the sharing of pleasure; shows men and women as equal sexual partners.

Nina Hartley, *Gauntlet*, vol. 2, 1997.

Harrison Voight, clinical psychologist and professor of human sexuality at the California Institute of Integral Studies in San Francisco, agrees.

"Women historically have had the strongest restraints and constraints taught to them by the culture," Voight says. "Women had to be in love all the time, to disdain sex for the sake of sex. Now women are getting close to a male style of sexuality."

Erotica Versus Porn

No one agrees about the definitions, but erotica is most often described as soft pornography and tends to include male and/or female nudity with simulated or soft-focus sex. Pornography is generally defined as depicting graphic sex with little attention to the back story. "Pornography is really hard core," Voight says. "Many critics argue that it more clearly objectifies women as sex objects. Erotica is designed to be a vivid portrayal of sexual activity, but the sex is not portrayed in a way that objectifies people."

However, others use the terms "erotica" and "porn" interchangeably. They say the differences between the two are non-existent. Erotica may just have nicer furniture than pornographic videos.

Hot Stuff, a sex supplies and video store in Santa Clara [California], tries to make women feel comfortable with open blinds, top-40 music and a women-only sales staff. Female customers stop in at lunch or after work to plan bachelorette parties, check out the accessories such as boas and buy videos. The most popular videos, says saleswoman Kristina Gomez, are ones that tell stories.

"I Like a Story"

Two women shopping together recently at Hot Stuff for lingerie giggled at the store's toys and sexually explicit greeting cards.

One, a 42-year-old from San Jose, says she began to watch pornography to indulge her husband. At first, it made her feel squeamish, she said. "I could never do that in front of a camera," she adds. But now she will watch it alone.

Another customer at Hot Stuff shopping for high-heeled shoes says she too was drawn into watching pornography by her boyfriend.

The Santa Clara woman, 46 and currently laid off from her technology sales job, says she watches videos alone at her boyfriend's house. But not at home—where her grown kids live with her. "I don't want to get busted," she says. "They are probably OK with it, but not for Mom."

The couple watches a range of pornography including stories with bondage, she says, "but nothing too twisted."

"I like classic porn." she says. "I like a story."

"Context" is what women want, says Carol Queen, staff "sexologist" at Good Vibrations, a cooperative of stores in San Francisco that sells sex toys, books and videos. "They want to know why are these two people or five people or 15 people having sex right now?"

For years, lesbian customers have been a pornography niche market. Now, straight, suburban females may represent a new market to retailers like Good Vibrations, which last year [2002] launched a national advertising campaign in mainstream magazines such as *Ladies' Home Journal*, *Cosmopolitan*, *Us* and *Marie Claire*.

Since then, mail-order and online business has increased 10 percent, says marketing manager Thomas Roche.

"There is an untapped market of women who won't go to video stores," says Anh Tran, who runs WantedList.com, an online service for ordering adult DVDs. "Reaching out and getting that market is where the real money is to be made."

What Women Watch

And what do women buy and watch? According to Roche, it's difficult to generalize, but women tend to like videos that focus on "natural-looking" women (those without breast implants). Women like to see women, not just men, enjoying sex. And female viewers like a positive attitude about women and sex.

Among female customers, top-selling videos are ones with strong female actors or with female directors. Some actresses have turned to directing, such as Veronica Hart, Candida Royalle and Chloe.

Of course, the debate over whether pornography is good or bad extends to women. Many therapists say they see no harm for either sex as long as it doesn't become a compulsion. Some raise questions with women about porno consumption as they would with men: Is it a way to escape? Is it about power? Or anger?

Others object to any pornography being available. "I would vigorously dispute that this stuff is beneficial to women," says Patrick McGrath, director of media relations at Morality in Media Inc., a New York–based organization that works to get federal and state obscenity statutes enforced. He said the pornography industry produces work that often portrays women in an offensive or degrading light. "I would question the efficacy of this material."

Violet Blue, author of . . . *The Ultimate Guide to Adult Videos*, agrees that the pornography industry has a lengthy record of making movies that denigrate women. "A lot of women have seen something that has turned them off," she says.

It's possible to avoid the offensive, Blue says, by finding out which movies are directed by women or have actors who have refused to be in movies with sexist stereotypes.

In the past five years, the number of female directors of pornographic video and film has increased from a handful to

30, compared to about 200 male porn directors.

Jewel De'Nyle, 27, is one of the newest pornography directors aiming for a wider market. A porn star too, she runs Platinum X Pictures, which makes some films targeted for women. Her No. 1 seller is *Dirty Girls*. "Guys enjoy it, lesbians enjoy it and straight married people enjoy it."

"Polyamory . . . is living by the principle that it is possible to love more than one person at a time without deception or betrayal."

Polyamory Is a Feasible Alternative to Monogamous Marriage

Valerie White

Polyamory is the practice of having more than one sexual relationship, with the knowledge and consent of all partners, explains Valerie White in the following viewpoint. She contends that polyamory is a healthy and ethical alternative to monogamous relationships, which many people find frustrating or difficult to maintain. Emphasizing the importance of trust, honesty, and loving communication rather than sexual variety, many polyamorous people form long-term intimate networks or group marriages, White points out. White, executive director of the Sexual Freedom Legal Defense and Education Fund, is a former vice president of the American Humanist Association.

As you read, consider the following questions:

1. What does White feel her relationship choices would be if not for polyamory?
2. How do polyamorous people cope with jealousy, according to the author?
3. What is the difference between swinging and polyamory, in White's opinion?

Valerie White, "A Humanist Looks at Polyamory," *The Humanist*, vol. 64, November/December 2004, pp. 17–20. Copyright © 2004 by the American Humanist Association. Reproduced by permission of the author.

There are two words that I apply to myself which, considered together, probably place me in one of the smallest categories of humanity. Those are polyamorous and Humanist. There is no way of knowing what percentage of the population engages in an open, responsible, and respectful multi-partner lifestyle, although it is likely that the number runs quite high and accounts for hundreds of thousands of people in the United States. But let's estimate that it's 2 percent (a number I found bruited about on the Internet), and that Humanists comprise less than 10 percent. That would put me in the class polyamorous Humanist, which comprises 0.2 percent of the general population. Of course, I think there is a correlation: I think it's probable that Humanists are more likely to be polyamorous and that polyamorists are more likely to be Humanist than the rest of the population.

I knew I was polyamorous and I knew I was Humanist before I knew the words.

Raised by atheist parents, I never had any god belief to lose and I've never acquired any, either. Being churchless in the 1950s wasn't an easy thing for a child to cope with, though, and it was with a sigh of homecoming that I discovered Unitarian Universalism [UU] when in college in 1962. I don't remember hearing the word Humanism until the mid 1980s, when my mother, who lived with me then, was a subscriber to the *Humanist*. I joined the American Humanist Association, publisher of the *Humanist*, on my own soon afterward. Ever since then that's what I've called myself.

What Is Polyamory?

I learned the word polyamory a few years later in 1994. . . .

I expect it would be useful for me to define polyamory, which is living by the principle that it is possible to love more than one person at a time without deception or betrayal.

I've known since my late teens that monogamy wasn't natural to me. Judging from the amount of garden variety cheating, swinging, and serial monogamy that goes on in our society, many many other people aren't naturally monogamous, either. I understand there may be people who, after they commit themselves to a partner, never feel a stirring of romantic or erotic interest in anyone else, but I'm not one of them. Heck, even Jimmy Carter admitted to lusting after other women in his heart.

"Well, of course" you say. "You can feel an attraction to someone besides your partner but you don't have to act on it." Maybe. An awful lot of people do act on it, however, and consequently a lot of marriages break up over adultery.

Without polyamory my choices would be:

1. cheat, lie, betray, deceive
2. engage in agreed-upon recreational sex, swapping with other couples
3. eschew committed relationships
4. embrace celibacy
5. chafe in resentful frustration

I find all five of these alternatives unacceptable. I live my life in a relationship in which each of us accepts that the other may have additional loving relationships. I can't imagine living any other way. This lifestyle is predicated upon the assumption espoused by Humanist science fiction writer Robert Heinlein that "love doesn't subtract; it multiplies." It is perhaps most melodically expressed in Humanist Malvina Reynolds' beloved song:

> Love is something if you give it away,
> Give it away, give it away.
> Love is something if you give it away;
> You end up having more.
>
> It's just like a magic penny;
> Hold it tight, and you won't have any;
> Lend and spend it, and you'll have so many
> They'll roll all over the floor.

Poly people believe that the deep, mutual love that glows in a longstanding relationship isn't necessarily destroyed by the energy that kindles in a new one.

The Biology of Polyamory

What is the biology of polyamory? Is it hardwired in the genes? Nobody knows. I suspect that many, perhaps most people, have the capacity to love multiple partners. An awful lot of people have had more than one lover. Many other species in the animal kingdom are poly, including humans' close cousins the bonobo chimpanzees. Even supposedly monogamous animals like swans turn out to hatch eggs fathered by multiple males.

In humans, however, is an instinctual drive for multiple partners only hardwired for males? Can it be true that the evolutionary advantage for men is to spread their seed as widely as possible and for women to cleave only to one? I doubt it. Why wouldn't it be evolutionarily advantageous for a woman to have more than one man who was willing to beat off saber-tooth tigers from her and her baby—and have a selection of men to mate with in pursuit of better offspring?

Love Enriches Love

To polyfolk, loving more than one partner comes as naturally as loving more than one child: you don't stop loving your firstborn when your next child comes along. In fact, you may feel that your first love is given new dimension when a new love enriches your life.

But a life of this kind requires honesty, openness, respect, self-confidence, trust, and, above all, communication. It's hard work. It can be painful. But I find it worthwhile. And it is completely congruent with my Humanist values. Doesn't choosing to love more than one person honestly and responsibly derive from these core Humanist principles found in Humanist Manifesto II of 1973?

We affirm that moral values derive their source from human experience. . . .

> Happiness and the creative realization of human needs and desires, individually and in shared enjoyment, are continuous themes of humanism. . . . We believe in maximum individual autonomy consonant with social responsibility. . . . While we do not approve of exploitive, denigrating forms of sexual expression, neither do we wish to prohibit, by law or social sanction, sexual behavior between consenting adults. The many varieties of sexual exploration should not in themselves be considered "evil". . . . Short of harming others or compelling them to do likewise, individuals should be permitted to express their sexual proclivities and pursue their lifestyles as they desire. We wish to cultivate the development of a responsible attitude toward sexuality, in which humans are not exploited as sexual objects, and in which intimacy, sensitivity, respect, and honesty in interpersonal relations are encouraged.

Humanist Manifesto III, published in 2003, adds:

Humans are social by nature and find meaning in relationships. Humanists long for and strive toward a world of mutual care and concern, free of cruelty and its consequences, where differences are resolved cooperatively without resorting to violence. The joining of individuality with interdependence enriches our lives, encourages us to enrich the lives of others, and inspires hope of attaining peace, justice, and opportunity for all.

To answer the question that everyone asks: yes, polyamorous people can get jealous. But we know that jealousy is the fear of losing something valued and so, when jealousy arises, all parties rally round to reassure the jealous one. Polyamorous people can also feel "compersion," taking joy from a beloved partner's pleasure with another love.

Forms of Polyamory

There are almost as many ways to practice polyamory as there are polyamorous people. Lots of people have one primary partner and one or more "secondary." Groups of people form an intimate network or a "group marriage." Poly people live in triads and quads and larger assemblies that are similar to the way traditional couples live. Popular mythology to the contrary notwithstanding, it appears there are as many male-female-male triads as the other way around.

Polyamory Is Not Swinging

There is a major distinction to be made between what is called "Swinging" and Polyamory. In swinging, the intent is to engage in non-monogamous sexual behavior without the development of love, affection or personal intimacy between oneself and the secondary partners. Swingers generally seek to engage in recreational sex without emotional intimacy. With polyamory, there is no such restriction, and the intent *is* to allow such emotional intimacy to exist, develop, and grow between the people involved.

"What Is Polyamory?" September 21, 2004, www.polyamory.com.

A subset of polyamory is polyfidelity, which is just what it sounds like; people practicing polyfidelity are sexually exclusive within their group. Polyamorous people can be heterosexual, bisexual, or homosexual. There are people practicing polyamory who are in their seventies and in their teens. In fact, there is some reason to believe that poly-style multi-partnering is the norm in the younger cohort.

There are almost as many reasons to be polyamorous as there are polyamorous people. Some people are poly simply because they want to have more sex. Some are poly because they want to have less. Some are poly because they love the excitement and energy of new relationships; some because they like the mutuality of group living. Some are poly because they don't find that one person can meet their emotional needs while others are poly because they don't want to be solely responsible for one person's emotional needs.

How did this movement (and it is a movement, with several national organizations, local support groups in most major cities, e-mail lists, matchmaking websites, and even a denominational UU group) get started and how did it get its name? The word polyamorous was coined by Morning Glory Zell in 1990 and is a hybrid of a Greek root meaning "many" and a Latin root meaning "love." Zell said she could have been consistently Latin or Greek and called it omni-amory or polyphilia, but they sounded like diseases.

Fictional Influences

In 1961 American science fiction writer Robert Heinlein wrote a novel entitled *Stranger in a Strange Land*. Its premise is that it's possible to love more than one person at a time: openly, honestly, spiritually, and sexually. While that idea wasn't exactly new (after all, there have been menages a trois in real life, in fiction, and in the movies for a long time), the concept fired the imaginations of lots of people in those years leading up to the 1967 summer of love, and a movement was born. Other novels by Heinlein, such as *The Moon Is a Harsh Mistress*, *Friday*, and *Time Enough for Love* are also cited by polyfolk as inspirational.

However, Heinlein and his fans weren't the only ones to be suggesting or advocating new ways of looking at relationships. Robert Rimmer's 1965 novel, *The Harrad Experiment*, and other novels also suggested that loving, committed, and respectful relationships don't have to be sexually exclusive.

Rimmer himself lived in a quad for many years with his wife and another couple. I had the honor once of meeting him and his wife; I discovered from talking to him that he valued his role as one of the fathers of the poly movement. When he died recently he was remembered as one of the founders of polyamory. Many people seized on Rimmer's premise and tried to create working multipartner relationships. The 1972 self-help book, *Open Marriage*, by George and Nina O'Neill contributed to the trend, even though many people found it curiously asexual.

In 1983 a study by Philip Blumstein and Pepper Schwartz reported that 15 to 28 percent of married couples in the sample group had "an understanding that allows non-monogamy" but weren't aware that other people were doing the same thing. It took the invention of the Internet to create the current explosive growth of the poly movement, as people who knew they wanted multiple relationships could finally find each other. (If you were to do a Google search on "polyamory" today you would get 75,000 hits.)

More About Love than Sex

Naturally, the thing most people think about when they learn of multipartner relationships is sex. When I was interviewed recently by a British women's magazine, the resulting article was balanced and fair but all the highlighted quotes were about sex. Intercourse is not the primary reason people seek polyamorous relationships. As a friend of mine once remarked, "Polyamory is about more love, not more sex." In fact, poly folk quip that they are too busy communicating and scheduling to have time for sex.

Sometimes it's easier to understand a concept by learning what it is not. Polyamory is not infidelity. Polyamory is not promiscuous, superficial, unthinking, irresponsible sex. Polyamory is not swinging. In my mind swinging is a perfectly responsible choice when neither party is coerced. But when swingers agree that they won't develop loving relationships with the people they swing with, swingers aren't polyamorous. When swingers do develop lasting, loving friendship with their swing partners I would say that what they're doing is indistinguishable from polyamory.

If you look for polyamory on the Internet you'll find that, like Humanism, there have been many attempts to define it. Most of them utilize words like ethical, responsible, honorable, open, honest, intentional, and principled.

I am a Humanist and I am polyamorous. I was both of these things before I had terms for them. I find my Humanism and my polyamory congruent and satisfying and I wouldn't part with either of them.

"State-sanctioned polyamory would spell the effective end of marriage."

Polyamory Would Destroy Monogamous Marriage

Stanley Kurtz

Polyamory—the practice of engaging in a stable sexual relationship with more than one person at a time—would destroy the traditional marriage and family if it were to become sanctioned by the state, argues Stanley Kurtz in the following viewpoint. In societies that have allowed the option of plural marriage, people tend to reject the idea of fidelity, he points out. Because such marriages do not uphold fidelity, they would be inherently unstable, easily broken, and damaging to children, he concludes. Kurtz is a research fellow at Stanford University's Hoover Institution.

As you read, consider the following questions:

1. What is one of the most common problems in polygamous and polyamorous relationships, according to Kurtz?
2. In the author's opinion, what are the roots of the U.S. polyamory movement?
3. What is the connection between swinging and polyamory, according to Kurtz?

Stanley Kurtz, "Beyond Gay Marriage," *Weekly Standard*, vol. 8, August 4–11, 2003, pp. 26–28. Copyright © 2004 by News Corporation, Weekly Standard. All rights reserved. Reproduced by permission.

After gay marriage, what will become of marriage itself? Will same-sex matrimony extend marriage's stabilizing effects to homosexuals? Will gay marriage undermine family life? A lot is riding on the answers to these questions. But the media's reflexive labeling of doubts about gay marriage as homophobia has made it almost impossible to debate the social effects of this reform. Now with the Supreme Court's ringing affirmation of sexual liberty in *Lawrence v. Texas*,[1] that debate is unavoidable.

Among the likeliest effects of gay marriage is to take us down a slippery slope to legalized polygamy and "polyamory" (group marriage). Marriage will be transformed into a variety of relationship contracts, linking two, three, or more individuals (however weakly and temporarily) in every conceivable combination of male and female. A scare scenario? Hardly. The bottom of this slope is visible from where we stand. Advocacy of legalized polygamy is growing. A network of grass-roots organizations seeking legal recognition for group marriage already exists. The cause of legalized group marriage is championed by a powerful faction of family law specialists. Influential legal bodies in both the United States and Canada have presented radical programs of marital reform. Some of these quasi-governmental proposals go so far as to suggest the abolition of marriage. The ideas behind this movement have already achieved surprising influence with a prominent American politician.

None of this is well known. Both the media and public spokesmen for the gay marriage movement treat the issue as an unproblematic advance for civil rights. True, a small number of relatively conservative gay spokesmen do consider the social effects of gay matrimony, insisting that they will be beneficent, that homosexual unions will become more stable. Yet another faction of gay rights advocates actually favors gay marriage as a step toward the abolition of marriage itself. This group agrees that there is a slippery slope, and wants to hasten the slide down.

To consider what comes after gay marriage is not to say that gay marriage itself poses no danger to the institution of

1. In this 2003 ruling, the Supreme Court struck down state laws banning sodomy.

marriage. Quite apart from the likelihood that it will usher in legalized polygamy and polyamory, gay marriage will almost certainly weaken the belief that monogamy lies at the heart of marriage. But to see why this is so, we will first need to reconnoiter the slippery slope.

Promoting Polygamy

During the 1996 congressional debate on the Defense of Marriage Act, which affirmed the ability of the states and the federal government to withhold recognition from same-sex marriages, gay marriage advocates were put on the defensive by the polygamy question. If gays had a right to marry, why not polygamists? Andrew Sullivan, one of gay marriage's most intelligent defenders, labeled the question fear-mongering —akin to the discredited belief that interracial marriage would lead to birth defects. "To the best of my knowledge," said Sullivan, "there is no polygamists' rights organization poised to exploit same-sex marriage and return the republic to polygamous abandon." Actually, there are now many such organizations. And their strategy—even their existence—owes much to the movement for gay marriage.

Scoffing at the polygamy prospect as ludicrous has been the strategy of choice for gay marriage advocates. In 2000, following Vermont's enactment of civil unions, Matt Coles, director of the American Civil Liberties Union's [ACLU's] Lesbian and Gay Rights Project, said, "I think the idea that there is some kind of slippery slope [to polygamy or group marriage] is silly." As proof, Coles said that America had legalized interracial marriage, while also forcing Utah to ban polygamy before admission to the union. That dichotomy, said Coles, shows that Americans are capable of distinguishing between better and worse proposals for reforming marriage.

Are we? When Tom Green was put on trial in Utah for polygamy in 2001, it played like a dress rehearsal for the coming movement to legalize polygamy. True, Green was convicted for violating what he called Utah's "don't ask, don't tell" policy on polygamy. Pointedly refusing to "hide in the closet," he touted polygamy on the Sally Jessy Raphael, Queen Latifah, Geraldo Rivera, and Jerry Springer shows, and on *Dateline NBC* and *48 Hours*. But the Green trial was not just a cable spectacle. It brought out a surprising number of mainstream defenses of polygamy. And most of the defenders went to bat for polygamy by drawing direct comparisons to gay marriage.

State-Sanctioned Promiscuity?

Writing in the *Village Voice*, gay leftist Richard Goldstein equated the drive for state-sanctioned polygamy with the movement for gay marriage. The political reluctance of gays to embrace polygamists was understandable, said Goldstein, "but our fates are entwined in fundamental ways." Libertarian Jacob Sullum defended polygamy, along with all other consensual domestic arrangements, in the *Washington Times*. Syndicated liberal columnist Ellen Goodman took up the cause of polygamy with a direct comparison to gay marriage. Steve Chapman, a member of the *Chicago Tribune* editorial board, defended polygamy in the *Tribune* and in *Slate*. The *New York Times* published a Week in Review article juxtaposing photos of Tom Green's family with sociobiological arguments about the naturalness of polygamy and promiscuity.

The ACLU's Matt Coles may have derided the idea of a slippery slope from gay marriage to polygamy, but the ACLU itself stepped in to help Tom Green during his trial and declared its support for the repeal of all "laws prohibiting or penalizing the practice of plural marriage." There is of course a difference between repealing such laws and formal state recognition of polygamous marriages. Neither the ACLU nor, say, Ellen Goodman has directly advocated formal state recognition. Yet they give us no reason to suppose that, when the time is ripe, they will not do so. Stephen Clark, the legal director of the Utah ACLU, has said, "Talking to Utah's polygamists is like talking to gays and lesbians who really want the right to live their lives."

All this was in 2001, well before the prospect that legal gay marriage might create the cultural conditions for state-sanctioned polygamy. Can anyone doubt that greater public support will be forthcoming once gay marriage has become a reality? Surely the ACLU will lead the charge.

Why is state-sanctioned polygamy a problem? The deep reason is that it erodes the ethos of monogamous marriage.

Despite the divorce revolution, Americans still take it for granted that marriage means monogamy. The ideal of fidelity may be breached in practice, yet adultery is clearly understood as a transgression against marriage. Legal polygamy would jeopardize that understanding, and that is why polygamy has historically been treated in the West as an offense against society itself.

In most non-Western cultures, marriage is not a union of freely choosing individuals, but an alliance of family groups. The emotional relationship between husband and wife is attenuated and subordinated to the economic and political interests of extended kin. But in our world of freely choosing individuals, extended families fall away, and love and companionship are the only surviving principles on which families can be built. From Thomas Aquinas through Richard Posner, almost every serious observer has granted the incompatibility between polygamy and Western companionate marriage.

Where polygamy works, it does so because the husband and his wives are emotionally distant. Even then, jealousy is a constant danger, averted only by strict rules of seniority or parity in the husband's economic support of his wives. Polygamy is more about those resources than about sex.

Polygamists Reject Fidelity

Yet in many polygamous societies, even though only 10 or 15 percent of men may actually have multiple wives, there is a widely held belief that men need multiple women. The result is that polygamists are often promiscuous—just not with their own wives. Anthropologist Philip Kilbride reports a Nigerian survey in which, among urban male polygamists, 44 percent said their most recent sexual partners were women other than their wives. For monogamous, married Nigerian men in urban areas, that figure rose to 67 percent. Even though polygamous marriage is less about sex than security, societies that permit polygamy tend to reject the idea of marital fidelity—for everyone, polygamists included.

Mormon polygamy has always been a complicated and evolving combination of Western mores and classic polygamous patterns. Like Western companionate marriage, Mor-

Encouraged by alternative weddings in other parts of the country, the mayor of Parched Flat, Utah, performs the marriage of Elmer Sturdley, his nine wives, and a goat (not pictured).

Wolverton. © 2004 by Monte Wolverton. Reproduced by permission.

mon polygamy condemns extramarital sex. Yet historically, like its non-Western counterparts, it de-emphasized romantic love. Even so, jealousy was always a problem. One study puts the rate of 19th-century polygamous divorce at triple the rate for monogamous families. Unlike their forebears, contemporary Mormon polygamists try to combine polygamy with companionate marriage—and have a very tough time of it. We have no definitive figures, but divorce is frequent. Irwin Altman and Joseph Ginat, who've written the most detailed account of today's breakaway Mormon polygamist sects, highlight the special stresses put on families trying to combine modern notions of romantic love with polygamy. Strict religious rules of parity among wives make the effort to create a hybrid traditionalist/modern version of Mormon polygamy at least plausible, if very stressful. But polygamy let loose in modern secular America would destroy our understanding of marital fidelity, while putting nothing viable in its place. And postmodern polygamy is a lot closer than you think.

Polyamory

America's new, souped-up version of polygamy is called "polyamory." Polyamorists trace their descent from the anti-monogamy movements of the sixties and seventies—everything from hippie communes, to the support groups that grew up around Robert Rimmer's 1966 novel *The Harrad Experiment*, to the cult of Bhagwan Shree Rajneesh. Polyamorists proselytize for "responsible non-monogamy"—open, loving, and stable sexual relationships among more than two people. The modern polyamory movement took off in the mid-nineties— partly because of the growth of the Internet (with its confidentiality), but also in parallel to, and inspired by, the rising gay marriage movement.

Unlike classic polygamy, which features one man and several women, polyamory comprises a bewildering variety of sexual combinations. There are triads of one woman and two men; heterosexual group marriages; groups in which some or all members are bisexual; lesbian groups, and so forth. (For details, see Deborah Anapol's *Polyamory: The New Love Without Limits*, one of the movement's authoritative guides, or Google the word polyamory.)

Supposedly, polyamory is not a synonym for promiscuity. In practice, though, there is a continuum between polyamory and "swinging." Swinging couples dally with multiple sexual partners while intentionally avoiding emotional entanglements. Polyamorists, in contrast, try to establish stable emotional ties among a sexually connected group. Although the subcultures of swinging and polyamory are recognizably different, many individuals move freely between them. And since polyamorous group marriages can be sexually closed or open, it's often tough to draw a line between polyamory and swinging. Here, then, is the modern American version of Nigeria's extramarital polygamous promiscuity. Once the principles of monogamous companionate marriage are breached, even for supposedly stable and committed sexual groups, the slide toward full-fledged promiscuity is difficult to halt.

The Polyamorist Rights Movement

Polyamorists are enthusiastic proponents of same-sex marriage. Obviously, any attempt to restrict marriage to a single man and woman would prevent the legalization of polyamory. After passage of the Defense of Marriage Act in 1996, an article appeared in *Loving More*, the flagship magazine of the polyamory movement, calling for the creation of a polyamorist rights movement modeled on the movement for gay rights. The piece was published under the pen name Joy Singer, identified as the graduate of a "top ten law school" and a political organizer and public official in California for the previous two decades.

Taking a leaf from the gay marriage movement, Singer suggested starting small. A campaign for hospital visitation rights for polyamorous spouses would be the way to begin. Full marriage and adoption rights would come later. Again using the gay marriage movement as a model, Singer called for careful selection of acceptable public spokesmen (i.e., people from longstanding poly families with children). Singer even published a speech by Iowa state legislator Ed Fallon on behalf of gay marriage, arguing that the goal would be to get a congressman to give exactly the same speech as Fallon, but substituting the word "poly" for "gay" throughout. Try telling polyamorists that the link between gay marriage and group marriage is a mirage.

The flexible, egalitarian, and altogether postmodern polyamorists are more likely to influence the larger society than Mormon polygamists. The polyamorists go after monogamy in a way that resonates with America's secular, post-sixties culture. Yet the fundamental drawback is the same for Mormons and polyamorists alike. Polyamory websites are filled with chatter about jealousy, the problem that will not go away. Inevitably, group marriages based on modern principles of companionate love, without religious rules and restraints, are unstable. Like the short-lived hippie communes, group marriages will be broken on the contradiction between companionate love and group solidarity. And children will pay the price. The harms of state-sanctioned polyamorous marriage would extend well beyond the polyamorists themselves. Once monogamy is defined out of marriage, it will be next to impossible to educate a new generation in what it takes to keep companionate marriage intact. State-sanctioned polyamory would spell the effective end of marriage. And that is precisely what polyamory's new—and surprisingly influential—defenders are aiming for.

"Almost all women working in prostitution use drugs and alcohol heavily . . . to deal with the stress and emotional issues of the trade."

Prostitution Is Harmful

Kari Lydersen

Many women who work as prostitutes have been involved in a cycle of exploitation that began in childhood, reports Chicago-based writer Kari Lydersen in the following viewpoint. A large percentage of prostitutes were sexually abused as children and never received any counseling to help them deal with the trauma, she notes. Believing that they can survive by selling their bodies, these women often become dependent on drugs, crime, and abusive relationships to cope with the difficulties of their lifestyle. Until American society confronts the rampant exploitation of women and children, prostitution will continue to be part of a dangerous cycle of abuse, Lydersen concludes.

As you read, consider the following questions:

1. According to Lydersen, why do some abused girls and women turn to prostitution?
2. According to a 2001 study cited by the author, what percentage of prostitutes have a first "date" before the age of eighteen?
3. What enables some prostitutes to leave their lifestyle, according to Lydersen?

Kari Lydersen, "Vicious Cycle: Shedding Light on a Cycle of Abuse," *In These Times*, vol. 28, December 8, 2003, pp. 20–21. Copyright © 2003 by *In These Times*, www.inthesetimes.com. Reproduced by permission.

Growing up on Chicago's South Side, Brenda Myers looked up to the prostitutes working outside her window. "I asked my grandmother what those women were doing. She said, 'They take their panties off for money.'"

At age 9 this idea didn't strike Myers as odd—a family member had been molesting her for years—and she grew up understanding that her body would be the way she got by: "I was thinking, well, they're already taking my panties off, and I wasn't getting any money. So I'll make them pay for it," she says.

She did, and like a majority of women working the streets, Myers became mired in a cycle of dependency on drugs, alcohol, prostitution and abusive relationships—a cycle that starts in youth and ends up landing them in jail and prison.

Women are the fastest growing segment of the incarcerated—more than 91,000 were in state and federal prisons in 2000 (a figure that does not include jails). While the number of incarcerated men grew by 77 percent between 1990 and 2000, the female population grew by 108 percent, according to U.S. Department of Justice [DOJ] statistics.

Like Myers, about half the women behind bars are there for nonviolent offenses, primarily prostitution- and drug-related violations and petty theft or fraud, according to the DOJ.

Childhood Experiences Loom Large

And like Myers, a significantly high number of them are victims of childhood sexual abuse. A recent study by the Chicago Coalition for the Homeless reported that 41 percent of women arrested for prostitution-related offenses in Cook County jail were sexually abused as children.

The Illinois Coalition Against Sexual Assault (ICASA) conducted a study in which 57 percent of women working as prostitutes in the state reported they were sexually abused as children. The study also found that more than 90 percent lost their virginity through assault, and 70 percent believed being sexually abused as children influenced their decision to become prostitutes.

Likewise, a 1995 study by the National Criminal Justice Reference Service found that people who were sexually abused as children are a whopping 27.7 times more likely than others to be arrested for prostitution.

Cycles of Abuse

As Myers describes, many prostitutes say they turned to paid dates as a way to take control of their sexuality after having had it taken from them. Others are forced into prostitution by their abusers—a 2001 study by the Center for Impact Research (CIR) noted that it is common for adults in particularly dire circumstances to force children into prostitution to pay rent or to buy drugs.

A number of women interviewed in Chicago tell similar stories of how they ended up in and out of jail on drug- and prostitution-related offenses. It starts with childhood sexual abuse by a relative or mother's boyfriend, a lifelong psychological trauma for which they often never receive counseling or treatment. Growing up in households where substance abuse and prostitution are prevalent, the women started both at a young age. According to the CIR study, 62 percent of prostitutes have their first "date" before age 18.

"My mother's ex-husband used to have me up in the middle of the night giving him head," says Louise Lofton, another former prostitute in Chicago, who has worked with Myers to form a group called Exodus to help women leave prostitution.

"One time she came in unexpectedly, and he started beating her because he knew he was in the wrong; he wanted to cover up for himself," Lofton says. "I ran into him once when I was in prostitution—I had this leopard print skirt on. I said, 'This is because of you.' He said, 'I'm sorry.' I said, 'F— you.'"

Untreated Addictions

Studies also show that almost all women working in prostitution use drugs and alcohol heavily. Many start using these substances or increase their usage in order to deal with the stress and emotional issues of the trade. Others begin to prostitute themselves to fund their drug habits or those of their partners or family members.

For many, the specter of sexual abuse lies behind it

all—driving them to seek solace or release in drugs and sex and complicating attempts to change their lives and recover.

Violence Against Women

Prostitution is not "sex work," it is violence against women. It exists because significant numbers of men are given social, moral, and legal permission to buy women on demand. It exists because pimps and traffickers prey on women's poverty and inequality. It exists because it is a last ditch survival strategy, not a choice, for millions of the world's women.

Janice G. Raymond, *Conscience*, Spring 2005.

"The drug abuse is just one part of it," says Tracy Banks-Geiger, the court and jail program coordinator at Genesis House, a free residential recovery program for women in prostitution in Chicago. "There are also issues of poverty, racism and childhood sexual abuse that never received any treatment."

Doing Harder Time

Women bear the brunt of prostitution incarcerations. Johns usually face heavy fines—under a Chicago city ordinance they are charged $700 in fines and car impoundment fees—but then, in the vast majority of cases, charges are dropped. Male pimps are likewise rarely arrested.

Along with this sexism, racism also plays in the challenges and threats faced by prostitutes. ICASA says that while 40 percent of street prostitutes are women of color, women of color constitute 55 percent of those arrested and 85 percent of those sentenced to jail time.

Dealing with sexual abuse and related traumas is key to breaking the cycle of incarceration and abuse. But most prisons and jails offer little in the way of support groups and counseling, and it can be even harder to access free resources once women get out.

Piecing Together a Life

In Chicago, several former prostitutes report that they were finally able to leave the lifestyle after finding support groups and programs that addressed both substance abuse and the physical and psychological issues involved in their early lives. Many women have had success at Genesis House, the only institution in the city accredited by the courts as an alternative to jail time. Genesis House is a strict yearlong residential program available free to walk-ins and women referred by the courts.

"They're very gentle and patient with me and don't rush me into anything," says a 32-year-old Genesis House resident who asked that her name not be used. "They're helping me build up all those things that had been ripped out of me by prostitution."

In general, recovering prostitutes and service providers have a tricky balance to keep. They need to avoid stigmatizing or condemning prostitution as a lifestyle choice and female sexuality as a whole while still acknowledging that, for many, prostitution is a piece of a painful puzzle they want to leave behind.

To break the cycle of sexual abuse, prostitution, drugs and incarceration, many women note that there must be fundamental change in a society that allows or even encourages the exploitation of children and women.

"If it wasn't for men you wouldn't have prostitution," Myers says. "They think it's a joke, she's having a ball. No she isn't! They think they didn't do anything wrong. Women need to be taught that their body isn't an offering or a sacrifice."

"Sex for money will happen no matter what. Why make it a criminal experience?"

Prostitution Should Be Legalized

Heidi Fleiss

Prostitution should be legalized and regulated, argues Heidi Fleiss in the following viewpoint. Drawing on her experience as a former prostitute and madam, Fleiss maintains that women should have the right to do what they want with their bodies. In addition, she contends, legalized prostitution would protect women from the kinds of abuses seen in the illegal sex-trade industry. With regulation, the government could collect taxes on the industry, and prostitutes would be required to use condoms and to test negative for sexually transmitted diseases. In 1993 Fleiss was arrested on charges of running a call-girl service in Los Angeles. She served three years in prison for money laundering, tax evasion, and attempted pandering.

As you read, consider the following questions:
1. What was Heidi Fleiss's childhood like?
2. Why did Fleiss become a madam?
3. What is the Daily Planet, according to the author?

Heidi Fleiss, "In Defense of Prostitution," *Legal Affairs*, vol. 2, September/ October 2003, pp. 35–36. Copyright © 2003 by *Legal Affairs*. Reproduced by permission.

[I]n 1993], I was arrested at my home in Beverly Hills for pandering, which the dictionary defines as acting as "a go-between in sexual intrigue." In other words, I was a madam. After a jury convicted me of three counts of pandering, the verdicts were thrown out, but the government didn't give up. It made me the Al Capone of prostitution. I spent three years in a federal penitentiary in Dublin, Calif., for conspiracy, tax evasion, and money laundering. But it was the sex that got me in trouble.

When I was a Hollywood madam, I had between 20 and 70 girls working for me and once made $97,000 in a single day on commissions. My take was 40 percent of whatever fee my girls received and of any tips over $1,000. (Compare that to prison, where I made about a dime an hour cleaning pots and taking out the trash.)

When I was in the sex trade, I ran an 85 percent cash business. I dealt with the richest people on earth—men who run countries and this country's top businesses. Most of them preferred to pay in cash. The actor Charlie Sheen was one of my few customers who wrote checks, but looking back I now realize he was a class act. He paid his bills, girls liked him, and he was well-endowed.

A Dream Childhood

I didn't get involved in prostitution because I needed money. I had the kind of childhood that everyone dreams about, with five brothers and sisters, camping trips, pillow fights, and marathon Monopoly games. We weren't like the Britney Spears generation—the girls today who look like they're ready to have sex at 9. I started a babysitting circle when I wasn't much older than that and soon all the parents in the neighborhood wanted me to watch over their children. Even then I had an innate business sense. I started farming out my friends to meet the demand. My mother showered me with love and my father, a pediatrician, would ask me at the dinner table, "What did you learn today?"

At 19, I began dating a 57-year-old multimillionaire. The relationship was good, but when it ended I realized that he had won every fight we had because I had no career, nothing to stand on. So I got a license in real estate. But before long,

I was wrapped up in an entirely different world. I began going to Helena's, a popular nightclub in Los Angeles run by Jack Nicholson's former housekeeper, and met a bookie who later introduced me to Madam Alex, a "businesswoman" whose employees were known for their good looks and popularity. (I didn't know at the time that I was there to pay off the guy's gambling debt.) I was expecting a sexy glamour queen like Faye Dunaway in the TV movie *Beverly Hills Madam*. But Madam Alex was a 5'3" bald-headed Filipina in a transparent muu muu. We hit it off.

My first john—I was then 22—was gorgeous. I would have slept with him for free if I had met him in a bar or on a blind date. We had a great night, and I made $3,000 after Madam Alex's 40-percent cut was deducted from my fee.

I'm glad I learned the business in the trenches, but my career as a hooker was short-lived. I'm not the California dream girl, and sexually, I'm lazy. The profession didn't play to my strengths, which lie in business, not bed. After Madam Alex and I had a falling-out in 1989, I decided to leave prostitution altogether and go back to college to become an art curator. (I had dropped out of junior college during my first semester when I was 17.)

Becoming a Madam

So why did I become a madam? I had tons of beautiful friends and lots of great connections from traveling the world with my ex-boyfriend. One day I just realized that I could run a sex business better than anyone else I knew. My first client was a Swiss businessman who was in Los Angeles with six acquaintances. I set the men up with some girls I knew and all of them were very happy. The word spread and demand snowballed after that. I tried to stay in college and run the business at the same time, but it was too hard skipping out of class to arrange get-togethers over the school's pay phone.

I would fly girls to meet clients in St. Tropez, London, or wherever they were in the world. Just from talking to a man, I knew what kind of girl he'd be interested in.

I made sure never to send a prostitute into an unsafe situation or one where she felt humiliated or degraded. I was always conscious of how prostitution could lower a woman's self-esteem and I didn't want anyone who worked for me to feel that way. My clients were some of the richest men in the world. They wanted to look the best and live the longest. They were at the doctor's regularly. I never had one girl come down with an STD [sexually transmitted disease], not even crabs. But I told my girls that if they ever felt uncomfortable with a client, they should call me and I would get them out of there—no matter where they were. I made my first million after only four months in the business.

A Woman's Right

I wouldn't recommend prostitution as a career because it doesn't have great long-term prospects. Still, a woman should have the right to do what she wants with her body. She might have a fantasy about becoming a prostitute; why shouldn't she act on it? Or she might need to do it for a month or two because she has no family, no money, nothing. The money could help her to do something positive with her life, like start a business or go to college. I remember a girl who came to me with choke marks around her neck. She was in an abusive relationship with her boyfriend and wanted me to help her get out of it. I recommended that she work at a restaurant for six months, but eventually I let her work for me. She made a quarter of a million her first time. She turned one more trick and then retired from the business to get a master's degree at UCLA.

Prostitution Should Be Legal

Prostitution should be legalized throughout the United States. The laws are currently written by and for men. I've been out of the business for 10 years, but I still hear stories of men who hit women, walk out without paying, or write checks to hookers and then stop payment. It's outrageous. Here's a woman who has performed a service to the best of her abilities and to her client's satisfaction. But nothing will happen to that client because he knows he won't be prosecuted for refusing to pay for sex. They go after the women in those cases, not the men.

There is no downside to legalizing prostitution. The government would benefit by collecting taxes on the industry. And regulation would clean up a lot of crime and help to protect women. Now, there are hotshot guys who beat up prostitutes and smack them around because they know they can get away with it. I remember some girls who approached me after working for illegal sex houses, "pussy factories." You wouldn't believe what went on in these places. A girl would stay at the factory and have sex with 5 to 10 guys every day for anywhere from $300 to $700 a pop. Some of the people running the factories would threaten the hookers and force them to stay. One girl told me that some guy gave her crack every morning so that she wouldn't make a fuss.

Potential Benefits of Regulated Prostitution

Third-party managed prostitution businesses should be required to provide condoms, spermicides, and other prophylactic materials to all employees engaged in sexual work, and to provide training in sexually transmitted disease prevention. In addition, third-party managed prostitution businesses should provide employees with health insurance that covers examination and treatment for sexually transmitted diseases.

Experienced sex workers who are ready to retire from active work as prostitutes could offer workshops on safe sex techniques—not only for new sex workers but for men and women who are interested in learning from the pros how to have great, safe sex.

Margo St. James and Priscilla Alexander, "Testimony on Prostitution," COYOTE, 2004, www.coyotela.org.

Prostitution doesn't have to be like that. I never ran a brothel in the traditional sense. I bought a one-story ranch house in Beverly Hills from Michael Douglas in 1991, and no sex for money took place at my home (except for one five-minute blow job given to a client in the bathroom by one of my girls—without my permission—for $5,000). My home was a place of comfort where the girls could talk shop. My front door was never locked. I had an Olympic-size pool and the girls would swim and sunbathe and fight about who gave the best blow jobs. They took pride in their work.

An Australian Bordello

In America, I went to jail for selling consensual sex. In Australia, I was asked to be an international ambassador of the first bordello to go on the stock exchange. The Daily Planet, founded in 1975 in Melbourne, went public [in May 2002], at 35 cents per share. One of the men who runs the Daily Planet, Andrew Harris, contacted me after seeing me on a late-night talk show and asked me to act as the company's international ambassador.

Prostitution was always technically legal in Australia. And since 1986, the State of Victoria (where Melbourne is) has become even more forward-thinking. Prostitutes can work in brothels, as long as they're not working in a residential area and the town says it's okay. And the law takes the pimps and the underworld out of the business. It prevents anyone convicted of a crime in the last five years from owning or managing a brothel. Employers can't employ prostitutes with STDs. And they can't play dumb. They have to make sure that the hookers test clean. They also have to provide condoms which, as we all know, can get kind of expensive.

The Daily Planet, initially valued at $5.5 million, has 150 working girls on its roster. Its stock has nearly doubled since May [2002]. The company supplies protective devices (condoms and dams) and makes sure the girls pass a blood check that shows they are healthy and free of drugs before they can work. The girls, who pay for their subsequent health checks, have to produce a certificate from a doctor each month guaranteeing their good health. Any sex that occurs inside the Daily Planet (even blow jobs) must be done with protection.

Working Girls

The Daily Planet, which operates out of an 18-room building that resembles a motel, does not directly employ the working girls and does not take a cut of what they make. The girls negotiate their fees and tips with their clients. The company makes its money by charging $115 per hour for the use of each room. Up to four girls can use a room at once, so on a good night a room can generate as much as $4,000 for the Daily Planet.

I met with about 60 of the girls when I was in Melbourne

[in May 2002]. The girls ranged in age from 19 to about 35, and the best ones made about $6,000 in a week. I told them that if they wanted to get good tips, the most important thing to stroke was a man's ego. I advised them not to support their boyfriends and not to buy drugs. I said that they should figure out their earning capacity, set a goal, meet it, and then move on. There's always someone younger and prettier who will come along and take their place.

The turnover rate at the Daily Planet is high. A handful of girls leave each week, but four times as many apply to take their place. You can't stop sex. And sex for money will happen no matter what. Why make it a criminal experience?

Periodical Bibliography

The following articles have been selected to supplement the diverse views presented in this chapter.

Alexander Cockburn — "Concerning Pee-Wee, Townshend, and Ritter," *Nation*, February 17, 2003.

David L. Delmonico and Elizabeth Griffin — "The Challenge of Treating Compulsive Sex," *Counselor*, August 2002.

Benoit Denizet-Lewis — "Double Lives on the Down Low," *New York Times Magazine*, August 3, 2003.

Stephen Fried — "One Woman's War on Sexual Slavery," *Glamour*, January 2005.

Amelia Grana — "Stepping Out of Stilettos: Porn for the Ladies: For Women, by Women," *Iris: A Journal About Women*, Spring 2002.

Teddy Harris — "Prostitution Should Be Legalized," *University Wire*, March 14, 2005.

Robert H. Knight — "Sacred Marriage Contract Only Has Room for Two," *Insight on the News*, June 8, 1998.

Kimberley Kreutzer — "Polyamory on the Left: Liberatory or Predatory?" *Off Our Backs*, May/June 2004.

Phelim McAleer — "Happy Hookers of Eastern Europe," *Spectator*, April 5, 2003.

Janice G. Raymond — "Sex Trafficking Is Not 'Sex Work,'" *Conscience*, Spring 2005.

Paul M. Rodriguez — "Virtual Child Porn's Very Real Consequences," *Insight on the News*, May 27, 2002.

Read Mercer Schuchardt — "Hugh Hefner's Hollow Victory: How the *Playboy* Magnate Won the Culture War, Lost His Soul, and Left Us with a Mess to Clean Up," *Christianity Today*, December 2003.

Andrew Sullivan — "Citizens—on Sodomy, the Court Gets It Right," *New Republic*, July 21, 2003.

Camille Williams — "Why the Law Should Discourage Some Sexual Practices," *World & I*, June 2004.

For Further Discussion

Chapter 1

1. Marjorie Ingall maintains that she is grateful for Alfred C. Kinsey's research on sexuality, but admits that she has some reservations about its influence on American culture. What are these reservations? In what ways do they differ from the reservations expressed by Sue Ellin Browder? Explain.

2. Ziauddin Sardar contends that the modern abandonment of sexual taboos and an increasing obsession with sex devoid of intimacy has led to "a decline in real sex." How do you think Vern L. Bullough would respond to Sardar's assertion? Use citations from the text in defending your answer.

3. Robert P. George and David L. Tubbs argue that the legalization of same-sex marriage will undermine traditional marriage by redefining the boundaries of marital relationships. Cynthia Tucker asserts that traditional marriage is being undermined by factors that have nothing to do with the promotion of gay marriage. What evidence do these authors present to support their conclusions? Which argument is more persuasive? Why?

Chapter 2

1. Robert Rector, Kirk A. Johnson, Jennifer Marshall, and J. Dennis Fortenberry each use data from the National Longitudinal Study on Adolescent Health in their arguments about the impact of teen virginity pledges. While Rector, Johnson, and Marshall contend that virginity pledges are beneficial, Fortenberry has serious reservations about their impact on public health. What do you think accounts for these authors' differences of opinion? Which author uses the health survey data to better effect?

2. Dorian Solot and Marshall Miller identify themselves as the founders of the Alternatives to Marriage Project, an organization that advocates for the rights of unmarried people. Stephanie Staal is the author of *The Love They Lost: Living with the Legacy of Our Parents' Divorce*. How does this information influence your assessment of their arguments about cohabitation? Explain.

3. After reading the viewpoints by Andrew Sullivan and the Alliance for Marriage, are you more or less likely to support a constitutional amendment that would define marriage as the union of a man and a woman? Why or why not?

Chapter 3

1. Compare this chapter's viewpoints about abstinence-centered sex education with the viewpoints on safe-sex education. What are the benefits and drawbacks of each? In your opinion, which sex education curriculum should American public schools endorse? Why?

2. Kevin Jennings argues that schools should confront antigay prejudice by actively encouraging respect for sexual minorities. Joan Frawley Desmond maintains that an emphasis on tolerance for gay and lesbian students often leads schools to endorse homosexuality. Do you believe that educational institutions should promote tolerance for sexual minorities? Why or why not? Support your answer with evidence from the viewpoints.

Chapter 4

1. Cite some of the evidence that Rebecca Hagelin uses to support her view that pornography is harmful. Do you find her evidence persuasive? If so, why? If not, what evidence provided by Manny Howard and Michelle Quinn do you find convincing?

2. Stanley Kurtz maintains that the movement for gay marriage is creating a "slippery slope" into advocacy for polyamory. How does he support this assertion? Is his logic sound? Why or why not?

3. Kari Lydersen contends that prostitution is often part of a cycle of exploitation involving women who had been sexually abused as children. Heidi Fleiss argues that prostitution gives a woman a chance to earn money that could "help her do something positive with her life." Do you believe prostitution should be legalized? Use citations from the viewpoints in defending your answer.

Organizations to Contact

Advocates for Youth
2000 M St. NW, Suite 750, Washington, DC 20036
(202) 419-3420 • fax: (202) 419-1448
e-mail: questions@advocatesforyouth.org
Web site: www.advocatesforyouth.org

Advocates for Youth is the only organization that works both in the United States and in developing countries with a sole focus on adolescent reproductive and sexual health. It provides information, education, and advocacy to youth-serving agencies and professionals, policy makers, and the media. Among the organization's numerous publications are the fact sheets "Adolescent Protective Behaviors: Abstinence and Contraceptive Use" and "GLBTQ Youth: At Risk and Underserved," and the report *Science and Success: Sex Education and Other Programs That Work to Prevent Teen Pregnancy, HIV, and Sexually Transmitted Infections.*

The Alan Guttmacher Institute
120 Wall St., 21st Fl., New York, NY 10005
(212) 248-1111 • fax: (212) 248-1952
e-mail: info@guttmacher.org • Web site: www.guttmacher.org

The institute works to protect and expand the reproductive choices of all women and men. It strives to ensure that people have access to the information and services they need to exercise their rights and responsibilities concerning sexual activity, reproduction, and family planning. The institute publishes the following bimonthly journals: *Perspectives on Sexual and Reproductive Health, International Family Planning Perspectives,* and the *Guttmacher Report on Public Policy.*

Alliance for Marriage (AFM)
PO Box 2490, Merrifield, VA 22116
(703) 934-1212 • fax: (703) 934-1211
Web site: www.allianceformarriage.org

The AFM is a nonprofit research and education organization dedicated to promoting traditional marriage and addressing the epidemic of fatherless families in the United States. AFM exists to educate the public, the media, elected officials, and civil society leaders on the benefits of marriage for children, adults, and society. AFM also promotes reforms designed to strengthen the institution of marriage. Its Web site includes links to editorials, video clips, and articles, including "Healthy Marriages Are Good Social Policy," and "Celebrating Marriages of Pure Gold."

Alternatives to Marriage Project (AtMP)

PO Box 1922, Albany, NY 12201
(518) 462-5600
Web site: www.unmarried.org

The AtMP is a nonprofit organization that advocates for equality and fairness for unmarried people, including people who choose not to marry, cannot marry, or live together before marriage. Its goal is to fight discrimination on the basis of marital status and to educate policy makers and the public about relevant social and economic issues related to marital status. Its Web site includes reports such as *Let Them Eat Wedding Rings: The Role of Marriage Promotion in Welfare Reform* and links to dozens of articles, including "Unwedded Bliss," and "Changing the Shape of the American Family."

Coalition for Positive Sexuality (CPS)

PO Box 77212, Washington, DC 20013-7212
(773) 604-1654
e-mail: cps@positive.org • Web site: www.positive.org

The Coalition for Positive Sexuality is a grassroots direct-action group formed in the spring of 1992 by high school students and activists. CPS works to counteract the institutionalized misogyny, heterosexism, homophobia, racism, and ageism that students experience every day at school. It is dedicated to offering teens education on sexuality and safe sex that is pro-woman, pro-lesbian/gay/bisexual, and pro-choice. CPS offers an online forum called "Let's Talk!" for teens to talk about sex.

Concerned Women for America (CWA)

1015 Fifteenth St. NW, Suite 1100, Washington, DC 20005
(202) 488-7000 • fax: (202) 488-0806
e-mail: mail@cwfa.org • Web site: www.cwfa.org

CWA works to strengthen marriage and the traditional family according to Judeo-Christian moral standards. It opposes abortion, pornography, and homosexuality. The organization publishes numerous brochures and policy papers as well as *Family Voice*, a monthly newsmagazine.

Eagle Forum

PO Box 618, Alton, IL 62002
(618) 462-5415 • fax: (618) 462-8909
e-mail: eagle@eagleforum.org • Web site: www.eagleforum.org

Eagle Forum, founded by conservative analyst Phyllis Schlafly, advocates traditional family values. It stresses chastity before marriage and fidelity afterward, opposes birth control and abortion, and warns teens and others about the dangers of pornography and sexually transmitted diseases. The forum publishes the monthly *Phyllis Schlafly Report* as well as various articles and brochures.

Family Research Council

801 G St. NW, Washington, DC 20001
(202) 393-2100 • (800) 225-4008
Web site: www.frc.org

The council is a research, resource, and educational organization that promotes the traditional family, which it defines as a group of people bound by marriage, blood, or adoption. It opposes schools' tolerance of homosexuality and condom distribution programs in schools. It also believes that pornography breaks up marriages and contributes to sexual violence. The council publishes numerous periodicals from a conservative perspective, including *Culture Facts*, a weekly report, and *Washington Watch*, a monthly newsletter.

Gay, Lesbian and Straight Education Network (GLSEN)

121 W. Twenty-seventh St., Suite 804, New York, NY 10001
(212) 727-0135 • fax: (212) 727-0254
e-mail: glsen@glsen.org • Web site: www.glsen.org

GLSEN works to ensure safe and effective schools where every child learns to respect and accept all people, regardless of sexual orientation or gender identity expression. GLSEN's online library holds many documents about creating safe schools, including "That's So Gay," "Not Alone: Being a Straight Ally," and "Is This the Right School for Us?"

The Heritage Foundation

214 Massachusetts Ave. NE, Washington, DC 20002-1999
(202) 546-4400 • fax: (202) 546-8328
e-mail: info@heritage.org • Web site: www.heritage.org

The Heritage Foundation is a public policy research institute that promotes the ideas of limited government and the free market system. The foundation supports traditional family values and abstinence-only sex education and opposes cohabitation and same-sex marriage. Among the foundation's numerous publications is its Backgrounder series, which includes "Government Spends $12 on Safe Sex and Contraceptives for Every $1 Spent on Abstinence," the analysis report "Facts About Abstinence Education" and the commentary "Safe Sex: Time to Abstain."

National Campaign to Prevent Teen Pregnancy

1776 Massachusetts Ave. NW, Suite 200, Washington, DC 20036
(202) 478-8500 • fax: (202) 478-8588
e-mail: campaign@teenpregnancy.org
Web site: www.teenpregnancy.org

The mission of the National Campaign to Prevent Teen Pregnancy is to reduce teenage pregnancy by promoting values and activities that are consistent with a pregnancy-free adolescence. The campaign publishes pamphlets, brochures, and articles such as "The Relationship Between Teenage Motherhood and Marriage" and "The Sexual Behavior of Young Adolescents," as well as fact sheets on teen attitudes, condom use, and pregnancy rates.

Planned Parenthood Federation of America (PPFA)

434 W. Thirty-third St., New York, NY 10001
(212) 541-7800 • fax: (212) 245-1845
e-mail: communications@ppfa.org
Web site: www.plannedparenthood.com

Planned Parenthood believes individuals have the right to control their own fertility without governmental interference. It promotes comprehensive sex education and provides contraceptive counseling and services through clinics across the United States. PPFA's publications include the brochures *A Young Woman's Guide to Sexuality, What If I'm Pregnant?* and *Is This Love? How to Tell If Your Relationship Is Good for You.*

The Polyamory Society

e-mail: locator1@polyamorysociety.org
Web site: www.polyamorysociety.org

The Polyamory Society is a nonprofit organization that promotes and supports the interests of individuals in multipartner relationships and families. The society works to educate nonpolyamorists about polyamory and to accurately represent and preserve polyamory as a relationship alternative for future generations. Its Web site includes links to a glossary, the *Polyamory Society Newsletter,* and *Loving More* magazine.

Sexuality Information and Education Council of the United States (SIECUS)

130 W. Forty-second St., Suite 350, New York, NY 10036-7802
(212) 819-9770 • fax: (212) 819-9776
e-mail: siecus@siecus.org • Web site: www.siecus.org

SIECUS is an organization of educators, physicians, social workers, and others who support the individual's right to acquire knowledge of sexuality and who encourage responsible sexual behavior. The council promotes comprehensive sex education for all children that includes AIDS education, teaching about homosexuality, and instruction about contraceptives and sexually transmitted diseases. Its publications include fact sheets, annotated bibliographies by topic, and the monthly *SIECUS Report.*

Society for the Scientific Study of Sexuality (SSSS)
PO Box 416, Allentown, PA 18105-0416
(610) 530-2483 • fax: (610) 530-2485
e-mail: thesociety@sexscience.org • Web site:
www.sexscience.org

The Society for the Scientific Study of Sexuality is dedicated to advancing knowledge of sexuality. The SSSS believes in the importance of quality research and the application of sexual knowledge in educational, clinical, and other settings. The society also sees as essential the communication of accurate information about sexuality to professionals, policy makers, and the general public. It publishes the "What Sexual Scientists Know" brochure series and the monthly *Journal of Sex Research.*

Teen-Aid
723 E. Jackson Ave., Spokane, WA 99207
(509) 482-2868 • fax: (509) 482-7994
e-mail: teenaid@teen-aid.org • Web site: www.teen-aid.org

Teen-Aid is an international organization that promotes traditional family values and sexual morality. It publishes a public school sex education curriculum, *Sex, Commitment, and Family,* stressing sexual abstinence before marriage.

Bibliography of Books

Louisa Allen — *Sexual Subjects: Young People, Sexuality, and Education.* New York: Palgrave Macmillan, 2005.

William J. Bennett — *The Broken Hearth: Reversing the Moral Collapse of the American Family.* New York: Doubleday, 2001.

Jane D. Brown, Jeanne R. Steele, and Kim Walsh, eds. — *Sexual Teens, Sexual Media: Investigating Media's Influence on Adolescent Sexuality.* Mahwah, NJ: L. Erlbaum, 2002.

James W. Button and Barbara A. Rienzo — *The Politics of Youth, Sex, and Health Care in American Schools.* New York: Haworth Press, 2002.

David Campos — *Sex, Youth, and Sex Education: A Reference Handbook.* Santa Barbara, CA: ABC-CLIO, 2002.

Mike Cleveland — *Pure Freedom: Breaking the Addiction to Pornography.* Newburyport, MA: Focus, 2002.

Jeffrey Escoffier — *Sexual Revolution.* New York: Thunder's Mouth Press, 2003.

Melissa Farley — *Prostitution, Trafficking, and Traumatic Stress.* New York: Haworth, 2004.

Heidi Fleiss — *Pandering.* Los Angeles: One Hour Entertainment, 2003.

Bruce Fleming — *Sexual Ethics: Liberal vs. Conservative.* Lanham, MD: University Press of America, 2004.

Maggie Gallagher — *The Case for Marriage: Why Married People Are Happier, Healthier, and Better Off Financially.* New York: Broadway Books, 2001.

Jonathan Gathorne-Hardy — *Sex, the Measure of All Things: A Life of Alfred C. Kinsey.* Bloomington: Indiana University Press, 2000.

J. Mark Halstead and Michael J. Reiss — *Values in Sex Education: From Principles to Practice.* New York: RoutledgeFalmer, 2003.

Nan D. Hunter, Courtney G. Juslin, and Sharon M. McGowan — *The Authoritative ACLU Guide to the Rights of Lesbians, Gay Men, Bisexuals, and Transgender People.* New York: New York University Press, 2004.

Janice M. Irvine — *Talk About Sex: The Battles over Sex Education in the United States.* Berkeley and Los Angeles: University of California Press, 2002.

Philip Jenkins — *Beyond Tolerance: Child Pornography Online.* New York: New York University Press, 2001.

Paula Kamen   *Her Way: Young Women Remake the Sexual Revolution.* New York: Broadway Books, 2002.

Davina Kotulski   *Why You Should Give a Damn About Gay Marriage.* Los Angeles: Advocate Books, 2004.

Judith Levine   *Harmful to Minors: The Perils of Protecting Children from Sex.* Minneapolis: University of Minnesota Press, 2002.

Arthur Lipkin   *Beyond Diversity Day: A Q and A on Gay and Lesbian Issues in Schools.* Lanham, MD: Rowman & Littlefield, 2004.

John R. Llewellyn   *Polygamy Under Attack: From Tom Green to Brian David Mitchell.* Scottsdale, AZ: Agreka Books, 2004.

David Loftus   *Watching Sex: How Men Really Respond to Pornography.* New York: Thunder's Mouth Press, 2002.

Meredith Maran and Angela Watrous, eds.   *50 Ways to Support Lesbian and Gay Equality: The Complete Guide to Supporting Family, Friends, Neighbors—or Yourself.* Maui, HI: Inner Ocean, 2005.

Josh McDowell   *Why True Love Waits: A Definitive Book on How to Help Your Youth Resist Sexual Pressure.* Carol Stream, IL: Tyndale, 2002.

Tina S. Miracle   *Human Sexuality: Meeting Your Basic Needs.* Upper Saddle River, NJ: Prentice-Hall, 2003.

Judith A. Reisman   *Kinsey: Crimes and Consequences: The Red Queen and the Grand Scheme.* Crestwood, KY: Institute for Media Education, 1998.

Ira L. Reiss and Albert Ellis   *At the Dawn of the Sexual Revolution: Reflections on a Dialogue.* Lanham, MD: AltaMira Press, 2002.

Wendy Shalit   *A Return to Modesty: Rediscovering the Lost Virtue.* New York: Free Press, 1999.

Dorothy Allred Solomon   *Predators, Prey, and Other Kinfolk Growing Up in Polygamy.* New York: W.W. Norton, 2003.

Dorian Solot and Marshall Miller   *Unmarried to Each Other: The Essential Guide to Living Together as an Unmarried Couple.* New York: Marlowe, 2002.

Michael A. Sommers and Annie Leah Sommers   *Everything You Need to Know About Virginity.* New York: Rosen, 2000.

Carla A. Stephens   *A Passion for Purity: Protecting God's Precious Gift.* Tulsa, OK: Harrison House, 2003.

Nadine Strossen — *Defending Pornography: Free Speech, Sex, and the Fight for Women's Rights.* New York: New York University Press, 2000.

Jeffrey S. Turner — *Dating and Sexuality in America: A Reference Handbook.* Santa Barbara, CA: ABC-CLIO, 2003.

Walter L. Williams and Yolanda Retter, eds. — *Gay and Lesbian Rights in the United States: A Documentary History.* Westport, CT: Greenwood, 2003.

Lauren F. Winner — *Real Sex: The Naked Truth About Chastity.* Grand Rapids, MI: Brazos Press, 2005.

Evan Wolfson — *Why Marriage Matters: America, Equality, and Gay People's Right to Marry.* New York: Simon & Schuster, 2004.

Index